hide this french phrase book

Berlitz Publishing

New York   Munich   Singapore

Hide This French Phrase Book

Contacting the Editors
Every effort has been made to provide accurate information in this publication, but changes are inevitable. The publisher cannot be responsible for any resulting loss, inconvenience or injury. We would appreciate it if readers would call our attention to any errors or outdated information by contacting Berlitz Publishing, 193 Morris Avenue, Springfield, NJ 07081, USA. email: comments@berlitzbooks.com

Second Printing: June 2007
Printed in Canada

Writer: Eve-Alice Roustang Stoller
Editorial Director: Sheryl Olinsky Borg
Senior Editor/Project Manager: Lorraine Sova
Assistant Editor: Emily Bernath
Cover and Interior Design: Wee Design Group, Blair Swick
Production Manager: Elizabeth Gaynor
Illustrations: Kyle Webster, Amy Zaleski

INSIDE

INTRO

So, you're going to a French-speaking country, huh? Well then, you'd better learn a couple of useful phrases. By "useful" we mean the lingo you need to hook up, check in, and hang out. This un-censored phrase book's got you covered with everything you need to speak cool French—saying hi, getting a room, spending your bucks, finding a cheap place to eat, scoring digits... and a helluva lot more. We've even thrown in a few totally offensive, completely inappropriate, and downright nasty terms—just for fun. You'll be able to easily spot these by looking for 🌡. Wanna know the best of the worst? Look for 🌡.

We've got your back with insider tips, too. Check these out for up-to-date info that'll help you maneuver around a French locale...

FACT   cool facts that may seem like fiction

the Scoop   tips on what's hot and what's not

yo!   info you've gotta know

Warning—this language can get you into trouble. If you wanna say it in public, that's up to you. But we're not taking the rap (like responsibility and liability) for any problems you could encounter by using the expressions in Hide This French Phrase Book. These include, but are not limited to, verbal and/or physical abuse, bar brawls, cat fights, arrest... Use caution when dealing with French that's hot!

SPEAK UP

We don't want you to sound like a loser when speaking French. So, to make it easy for you, we've provided really simple phonetics (those are the funky letters right under the French expressions) with every entry you could say out loud. Just read the phonetics as if they're English, e.g.,

What's up?   ← *This is English, obviously.*

Quoi de neuf?   ← *A very cool French expression…*

kwah duh nuhf   ← *Say this as if it's English. Easy, right?!*

feeling nasal?

You get to make some cool nasal sounds when speaking French. In the phonetics, they're noted as (vowel) + N. Don't pronounce that "N" strongly; it's there to show the nasal quality of the previous vowel. Make that nasal sound by pronouncing the vowel through the mouth and the nose—at the same time. Fun!

not-so-dangerous liaison

Most final consonants aren't pronounced in French. But, if the word ending in a consonant is followed by a word beginning with a vowel, you should run them together—say the final consonant as if it's the first letter of the next word. For example, "nous" sounds like "noo" but "nous avons" sounds like "noo zavawN".

sex

Meaning gender… Words in French can be masculine or feminine. You'll see ♂ for masculine words, ♀ for the ladies.

Yeah, baby! Now you're ready for some French action.

THE BASICS

hi there

Make a good impression on the locals from the get-go.

Hello!
Bonjour!
bohN zhoor
Formal yet friendly.

Hi!
Salut!
sah-lew
Cute and to the point.

Hi, how are you?
Salut, ça va?
sah-lew sah vah
Drop the "salut" as an alternate greeting.

Good evening.
Bonsoir.
bohN swah

how're you doin'?

Ask about someone's well-being.

How are you?
Ça va?
sah vah
It's the quick way to say "Comment ça va?"

What's up?
Quoi de neuf?
kwah duh nuhf
Literally: What's new?

How's it going?
Ça boume?
sah boom
Literally: Is it blasting? "Boum" is the sound of a French explosion.

1

Doing well?	**Ça gaze?**
	sah gahz
	Literally: Is it gazing?

hey you!

Wanna get someone's attention? Try these.

Excuse me!	**Excusez moi!**
	ex-kew-zay mwah
	Not to be used as an apology.

Sir! / Ma'am!	**Monsieur ♂! / Madame ♀!**
	muh-sewr / mah-dahm
	Use this when you wanna be polite.

Yo!	**Hé!**
	eh
	A quick way to get someone's attention.

| Hey! | **Hep!** |
| | *ep* |

FACT In formal situations, it's best to address someone with "monsieur", sir; "madame", ma'am or madam; or "mademoiselle", miss. If you're with French friends, feel free to use "tu", the informal form of you. You should use "vous" with everyone else; it's the formal way to say you and is also the plural of "tu".

sorry

Oops…need to apologize?

My bad.	**Excuse.** *ex-kews*
Excuse me!	**Pardon!** *pah-dohN*
Sorry!	**Désolé ♂ / Désolée ♀ !** *day-zo-lay*

huh?

What did he or she just say? Make sure you understood it correctly.

Do you speak English?	**Parlez-vous anglais?** *pah-lay voo ahN-glay* *It's OK to ask if he or she speaks English.*
What was that?	**Qu'avez-vous dit?** *kah-vay voo dee*
Could you spell it?	**Pourriez-vous l'épeler?** *poor-ee-ay voo lay-play*

Please write it down.	**Pourriez-vous l'écrire, s'il vous plaît?**
	poor-ee-ay voo lay-kreer seel voo pleh
Can you translate this for me?	**Pourriez-vous me traduire ça?**
	poor-ee-ay voo muh trah-dweer sah
I (don't) understand.	**Je (ne) comprends (pas).**
	zhuh (nuh) kohN-prahN (pah)
Do you understand?	**(Est-ce que) vous comprenez?**
	(ess kuh) voo cohN-pruh-nay
	Let's hope someone has a clue as to what's going on!

help

Got yourself into a sticky situation?

Can you help me?	**Est-ce que vous pouvez m'aider?**
	ess kuh voo poo-vay may-day
Help!	**Au secours!**
	oh suh-koor
Call the police!	**Appelez la police!**
	ahp-lay la poleess
Stop thief!	**Au voleur!**
	oh vo-luhr
Fire!	**Au feu!**
	oh fuh
I'm lost.	**Je suis perdu ♂ / perdue ♀.**
	zhuh swee pair-dew
Get a doctor!	**Allez chercher un médecin!**
	ah-lay sher-shay aN made-saN

emergency

Just in case you get into trouble.

Where's the nearest police station?	**Où est le commissariat le plus proche?** *oo eh luh kum-ee-sah-ree-yah luh plew prawsh*
I want to report …	**Je veux signaler …** *zhuh vuh seen-yah-lay*
an accident.	**un accident.** *aN nahk-see-dahN*
an attack.	**une attaque.** *ewn ah-tak*
a mugging.	**une agression.** *ewn ah-gres-see-ohN*
a rape.	**un viol.** *aN vee-awl*
a theft.	**un cambriolage.** *aN kahN-bree-oh-lahzh*
I've been robbed.	**J'ai été volé ♂ / volée ♀.** *zhay ay-tay voh-lay*
I've been mugged.	**J'ai été agressé ♂ /agressée ♀.** *zhay ay-tay ah-gres-say*
I need to contact the consulate.	**Je dois contacter le consulat.** *zhuh dwah kohN-tahk-tay luh kohN-sew-lah*

 To get the police in an emergency, dial 17 in France, 101 in Belgium, 117 in Switzerland, and 911 in Canada.

bye-bye

From classic to cool, here are the best ways to say good-bye.

Good-bye.	**Au revoir.** *oh ruh-vwah*
Bye!	**Ciao! / Tchao!** *tchow* *Spell this popular Italian word the authentic way, "ciao" or the French way, "tchao".*
See you later.	**À plus.** *ah plew* *It's short for "à plus tard", see you later.*
See you soon.	**À tout.** *ah too* *This is a quick, cute way to say "à tout à l'heure", literally, within the hour.*
Good night.	**Bonne nuit.** *bohN nwee* *Say it when it's bedtime.*

by plane

Just arrived? Going somewhere? Act like you know what you're doing.

To …, please.	**À …, s'il vous plaît.**
	ah … seel voo pleh
	Top spots include Paris (of course), Côte d'Azur, and Provence, France and Montreal, Canada.

One-way. / Round-trip.	**Aller-simple. / Aller-retour.**
	ah-lay saN-pluh / ah-lay ruh-toor

How much?	**Combien ça coûte?**
	kohN-byaN sah coot
	Quick and to the point.

Are there any discounts?	**Y a-t-il des réductions?**
	ee a teel day ray-dewk-see-ohN
	Doesn't hurt to ask!

When is the … flight to …?	**À quelle heure est le … vol pour …?**
	ah kel uhr eh luh … vul poor

first	**premier**
	pruh-myay

next	**prochain**
	pro-shaN

last	**dernier**
	dehr-nyay

I'd like … ticket(s).	**Je voudrais … billet(s).**
	zhuh voo-dray … bee-yay

one	**un**
	aN

two	**deux**
	duh

Is there any delay on flight …?	**Est-ce que le vol … a du retard?** *ess kuh luh vul … ah dew ruh-tahr*
How late will it be?	**Il a combien de retard?** *eel ah kohN-byaN duh ruh-tahr*
Which gate does flight … leave from?	**De quelle porte part le vol …?** *duh kel pawrt pah luh vul*
Where is / are …?	**Où est / sont …?** *oo eh / sohN*
the baggage check	**la consigne** *la cohN-seen-yuh*
the luggage carts	**les chariots à bagages** *lay shah-ree-oh ah bah-gahzh*

Need cheap airline tickets? Do your research online. It's not only sites like cheaptickets.com, expedia.com, orbitz.com that offer great fares and package deals; you should also check out airline sites for special promotions. If that seems like too much work, it doesn't hurt to have someone do the work for you—call a travel agent for help. A fee for research usually won't be charged.

in flight

Sit back (if possible) and enjoy.

Can I have a blanket / pillow?	**Puis-je avoir une couverture / un oreiller?**
	pwee zhuh ah-vwa ewn koo-vair-tewr / aN nor-ay-ay
I ordered a … meal.	**J'ai commandé un plat …**
	zhay cohN-mahN-day aN plah
diabetic	**pour diabétiques.**
	poor dee-ah-bay-teek
gluten free	**sans gluten.**
	sahN glew-ten
kosher	**cacher.**
	kah-shay
low calorie / cholesterol / fat / sodium	**pauvre en calories / cholestérol / graisses / sodium.**
	poh-vruh ahN kah-loh-ree / koh-les-tair-awl / gress / soh-dyum
vegetarian	**végétarien.**
	vay-zhay-tah-ree-eN
I need a barf bag.	**J'ai besoin d'un sachet pour vomir.**
	zhay buh-zwaN daN sah-shay poor vo-meer
	Gross.

your stuff

Find it, grab it, and go!

Where is the luggage from flight …?	**Où sont les bagages du vol …?**
	oo sohN lay bah-gazh dew vul

My luggage has been stolen.	**On m'a volé mes bagages.** *ohN mah voh-lay may bah-gazh*
My suitcase was damaged.	**Ma valise a été abîmée.** *mah vah-leez ah ay-tay ah-bee-may* *In other words: Someone's gonna pay for this!*
Our luggage hasn't arrived.	**Nos bagages ne sont pas arrivés.** *noh bah-gazh nuh sohN pah zah-ree-vay* *What a nightmare.*

Just arrived in Paris? The most reliable way to get from Roissy / Charles-de-Gaulle Airport to the city center is by train. It runs every 15 minutes from 5 a.m. to 11:45 p.m. from terminal 2. You could take a bus or taxi, but traffic in Paris can be a nightmare; the trip could take anywhere from 30 minutes to over an hour!

by train

OK, first, you gotta get there.

How do I get to the (main) train station?	**Pour aller à la gare (principale)?** *poor ah-lay ah lah gah (praN-see-pahl)*
Is it far?	**(Est-ce que) c'est loin?** *(ess kuh) seh lwaN*

 Paris has several main stations—so don't go to the wrong one! "Gare du Nord" is north Paris; you can grab the Eurostar train to the UK from here. "Gare de l'Est" is east Paris; "Gare d'Austerlitz" is southwest Paris and offers service to Bordeaux, France, and Spain; "Gare Saint-Lazare" provides access to Normandy and Dieppe; "Gare Montparnasse" is west Paris and includes service to Brittany; and "Gare de Lyon" has trains that go to the French Riviera as well as Switzerland and Italy.

waitin' for the train

Learn to negotiate your way around the station.

Where is / are …?	**Où est / sont …?** *oo eh / sohN*
the bathroom	**les toilettes** *lay twah-let*
the currency exchange office	**le bureau de change** *luh bew-roh duh shahnzh*
the baggage check	**la consigne** *lah kohN-seen-yuh*
the lost-and-found	**le bureau des objets trouvés** *luh bew-roh day zob-zhay troo-vay*
the luggage lockers	**la consigne automatique** *lah cohN-seen-yuh oh-toh-mah-teek*
the platforms	**les quais** *lay kay*
the snack bar	**le snack-bar / buffet** *luh snahk bahr / bew-feh*

Where is / are …?	**Où est / sont …?**
	oo eh / sohN
the ticket office	**le guichet**
	luh gee-shay
the waiting room	**la salle d'attente**
	lah sahl dah-tahNt
Where can I buy a ticket?	**Où puis-je acheter un billet?**
	oo pwee zhuh ahsh-tay aN bee-yay
I'd like a … (ticket) to …	**Je voudrais un … pour …**
	zhuh voo-dray aN … poor
one-way	**aller-simple**
	ah-lay saN-pluh
round-trip	**aller-retour**
	ah-lay ruh-toor
How much is that?	**Combien ça coûte?**
	kohN-byaN sah koot
Is there a discount for students?	**Y a-t-il une réduction pour les étudiants?**
	ee a teel ewn ray-dewk-see-ohN poor ay-tew-dyahN
Do you offer a cheap same-day round-trip ticket?	**Est-ce que vous offrez un aller-retour à prix réduit dans la même journée?**
	es kuh voo zawf-ray aN nah-lay-ruh-toor ah pree ray-dwee dahN lah mem zhoor-nay
Could I have a schedule?	**Est-ce que je pourrais avoir les horaires?**
	ess kuh zhuh poor-ay ah-vwah lay zoh-rai
How long is the trip?	**Combien de temps dure le voyage?**
	kohN-byaN duh tahN dewr luh vwah-yahzh

When is the ... train to ...?	**À quelle heure est le ... train pour ...?**
	ah kel uhr eh luh ... traN poor
first	**premier**
	pruh-myay
next	**prochain**
	proh-shaN
last	**dernier**
	dairn-yay

train talk

Whether you're waiting for the train or looking for a seat, make conversation with a good-looking French guy or girl.

Hello you. Where is platform ...?	**Bonjour vous. Où est le quai numéro ...?**
	bohN zhoor voo oo eh luh kay new-mair-oh
Is this the train to ...?	**Est-ce que c'est bien le train pour ...?**
	ess kuh seh byaN luh traN poor
	I bet you're hoping he/she will be on your train.
Is this seat taken?	**Est-ce que cette place est occupée?**
	ess kuh set plahss eh taw-kew-pay
	It may be a long ride—find someone to enjoy it with.
Do you mind if I sit here?	**Est-ce que ça vous dérange si je m'asseois ici?**
	ess kuh sah voo day-rahNzh see zhuh mah-swah ee-see
	Get a little closer.

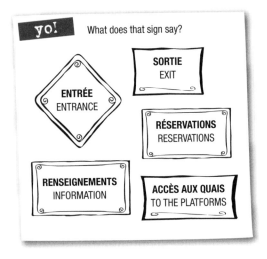

yo! What does that sign say?

SORTIE EXIT

ENTRÉE ENTRANCE

RÉSERVATIONS RESERVATIONS

RENSEIGNEMENTS INFORMATION

ACCÈS AUX QUAIS TO THE PLATFORMS

the scoop

Taking the train can be cheap if you take advantage of the many discounts available. If you're under 26, check out the Eurail Youthpass, which allows you to travel by train at a reduced rate in and outside of France. Traveling as a couple? Since France is for lovers, you can get a "Carte couple" for special train discounts. If you don't fit either of these categories, try traveling during off-peak hours to save a few euros.

Now that you've got your ticket, don't forget to validate it using the orange automatic date-stamping machine—labeled "composter votre billet"—at the entrance to the platform. If you don't, you'll be fined. This goes for the Métro and bus, too!

by bus

It's not always the fastest way to get around, but it sure beats walking!

Where is the bus station?	**Où est la gare routière?** *oo eh lah gah roo-tyehr*
Where can I buy tickets?	**Où est-ce que je peux acheter des tickets?** *oo ess kuh zhuh puh ahsh-tay day tee-keh*
A one-way / round-trip ticket to …	**Un ticket aller / aller-retour pour …** *aN tee-keh ah-lay / ah-lay ruh-toor poor*
A booklet of tickets.	**Un carnet de tickets.** *aN kahr-neh duh tee-keh* *The "carnet" includes 10 tickets at a discounted price. What a deal!*
How much is the fare to …?	**Combien coûte un ticket pour …?** *kohN-byaN koot aN tee-keh poor*
Is this the right bus to …?	**C'est bien le bon bus pour …?** *seh byaN luh bohN bewss poor*
Could you tell me when to get off?	**Pourriez-vous me dire quand il faut descendre?** *poor-ee-ay voo muh deer kahN teel foh day-sahN-druh* *Just in case you have no clue as to where you're headed…*
Next stop, please!	**Prochain arrêt, s'il vous plaît!** *pro-shaN nah-reh seel voo pleh* *If you want the driver to stop, better say please!*

by subway

Is goin' underground your style? Then you'll need these.

Where's the nearest
subway station?

**Où est la station de Métro
la plus proche?**

*oo eh lah stah-see-ohN duh may-troh lah
plew prawsh*

Please let it be in walking distance.

Where can I buy a ticket?

**Où est-ce que je peux acheter un
ticket?**

oo ess kuh zhuh puh ahsh-tay aN tee-keh

Could I have a map
of the subway?

**Est-ce que je pourrais avoir
un plan du Métro?**

*ess kuh zhuh poor-ay ah-vwah aN plahN
dew may-troh*

*If you ask nicely, you may
actually get what you want.*

Which line should I
take for …?

**Quelle ligne dois-je prendre
pour …?**

kel leen-yuh dwah-zhuh prahN-druh poor

*If the subway map is incompre-
hensible, ask a cutie for help.*

Is the next stop …?

**Est-ce que la prochaine station
est bien …?**

*ess kuh lah proh-shen stah-see-ohN
eh byaN*

Where are we?

Où sommes-nous?

oo sum noo

Don't have a clue, huh?!

 If you want to bump and grind with Parisians, the "Métro", subway, is the place to do it—around 9 million people take the Métro daily. It's easy to navigate once you grab a free Métro map, available at every Métro station. And, since the train runs from 5:30 a.m. to 12:30 a.m., you'll have plenty of time to familiarize yourself with the subway system.

Should you happen to be in Montreal, Canada, you can hop on the very clean and efficient Métro at any one of 65 stations throughout the city anytime between 5:30 a.m. and 1 a.m. Buy a strip of six tickets to get a discount; you can also get day and monthly passes. Free subway maps are available at ticket booths.

by taxi

Feelin' lazy? Get a cab.

Where can I get a taxi?	**Où est-ce que je peux trouver un taxi?** *oo ess kuh zhuh puh troo-vay aN tahx-ee*
Please take me to …	**Emmenez-moi à …, s'il vous plaît.** *ahN-muh-nay mwah ah … seel voo pleh*
a good bar.	**un bar sympa** *aN bah saN-pah*
a good club.	**une boîte sympa** *ewn bwaht saN-pah*
the airport.	**l'aéroport** *lah-air-oh-paw*
the train station.	**la gare** *lah gah*
this address.	**cette adresse** *set ah-dress*

How much is that?	**Combien ça coûte?** *kohN-byaN sah koot*
Keep the change.	**Gardez la monnaie.** *gah-day lah moh-nay*

FACT Many French taxis will take only three people because passengers aren't usually allowed to sit in the front seat. If you call a taxi in advance, you'll be picked up with the meter already running. Wanna know how much to tip the cabbie? It varies by country/city. France: 10–15%; Belgium: optional; Switzerland: 15% (sometimes included); Quebec City and Montreal: 10–15%.

by car

Can't give up the luxury of having your own car?

Where can I rent a car?	**Où est-ce que je peux louer une voiture?** *oo ess kuh zhuh puh loo-ay ewn vwah-tewr*
I'd like to rent …	**Je voudrais louer …** *zhuh voo-dray loo-ay*
an automatic.	**une voiture automatique.** *ewn vwah-tewr oh-toh-mah-teek*
a car with air conditioning.	**une voiture avec climatisation** *ewn vwah-tewr ah-vek klee-mah-te* *zah-see-ohN*

| How much does it cost per day / week? | **Quel est le tarif par jour / semaine?** |
| | *kel eh luh tah-reef pahr zhoor / suh-men* |

| Is mileage / insurance included? | **Est-ce que le kilométrage / l'assurance est compris ♂ / comprise ♀ ?** |
| | *ess kuh luh kee-loh-meh-trazh / lah-sew-rahNss eh cohN-pree / cohN-preez* |

| Where's the next gas station? | **Où est la station-service la plus proche?** |
| | *oo eh lah stah-see-ohN sair-veess lah plew prawsh* |

| Is it self-service? | **Est-ce que c'est un self-service?** |
| | *ess kuh set aN self-sair-veess* |

| Fill it up, please. | **Le plein, s'il vous plaît.** |
| | *luh plen seel voo pleh* |

car trouble

Having a breakdown?

| My car broke down. | **Ma voiture est tombée en panne.** |
| | *mah vwah-tewr eh tohN-bay ahN pahn* |

| Can you send a mechanic / tow truck? | **Pouvez-vous m'envoyer un mécanicien / une dépanneuse?** |
| | *poo-vay voo mahN-vwah-yay aN may-kahn-ee-see-aN / ewn day-pahn-uhz* |

I've run out of gas.	**Je suis en panne d'essence.**
	zhuh swee zahN pahn des-sahNss
	Duh!

| I have a flat. | **J'ai un pneu à plat.** |
| | *zhay aN pnuh ah plah* |

I've locked the keys
in the car.

J'ai fermé mes clés dans la voitur
zhay fair-may may klay dahN lah vwah-te
Nice one.

yo! Ready for a road trip? American, Australian,
and British licenses are valid in France and
Quebec Province, Canada. Signs in both are in French, of course.
You may see these signs:

Cédez le passage
Give way

Vous n'avez pas la priorité
You do not have the right of way

Passage protégé
No right of way

Priorité à droite
Give way to the right

auto wreck

If you get pulled over or worse, these expressions may help.

He / She ran into me.

**Il / Elle m'est rentré♂ / rentrée♀
dedans.**
eel / el meh rahN-tray duh-dahN

He / She was driving
too fast / too close.

**Il / Elle conduisait trop vite /
trop près.**
eel / el kohN-dwee-zay troh veet / troh pr

I didn't see the sign.

Je n'ai pas vu le panneau.
zhuh nay pah vew luh pah-noh
Excuses, excuses.

by bike

Calling all bikers.

I'd like to rent …	**Je voudrais louer …** *zhuh voo-dray loo-ay*
a bicycle.	**un vélo.** *aN vay-loh*
a moped.	**une mobylette.** *ewn moh-bee-let* *Also called "vélomoteurs" and* *"cyclomoteurs".*
a motorbike.	**une moto.** *ewn moh-toh*
How much does it cost per day / week?	**Ça coûte combien par jour / semaine?** *sah koot kohN-byaN pahr zhoor / suh-men* *Don't get screwed; confirm the* *price in advance.*

by thumb

Hitchhiking is NOT recommended.

Where are you heading?	**Où allez-vous?** *oo ah-lay voo*
Is that on the way to …?	**Est-ce que c'est sur la route de …?** *ess kuh seh sewr lah root duh*
Could you drop me off here / at …?	**Est-ce que vous pourriez me déposer ici / à …?** *ess kuh voo poo-ree-ay muh day-poh-zay ee-see / ah*

get cash

Get your euros (France, Belgium), francs (Switzerland), or Canadian dollars and start spending your money!

Where's the nearest bank? **Où est la banque la plus proche?**
oo eh lah bahNk lah plew prawsh

Can I exchange foreign currency here? **Est-ce que je peux changer des devises étrangères ici?**
ess kuh zhuh puh shahN-zhay day duh-veez ay-trahnN-zhair ee-see

I'd like to change some dollars / pounds into euros. **Je voudrais changer des dollars / livres en euros.**
zhuh voo-dray shahN-zhay day doh-lah / lee-vruh ahN uh-roh

I want to cash some travelers checks. **Je voudrais encaisser des chèques de voyage.**
zhuh voo-dray ahN-kes-say day shek duh vwah-yahzh

What's the exchange rate? **Quel est le taux (de change)?**
kel eh luh toh (duh shahNzh)

ATM

Get cash fast.

Where are the ATMs [cash machines]? **Où sont les distributeurs automatiques?**
oo sohN lay dee-stree-bew-tuhr oh-toh-mah-teek

25

Can I use my card in the ATM?	**Est-ce que je peux me servir de m̶ carte dans ce distributeur?**
	ess kuh zhuh puh muh sair-veer duh ma̶ kahrt dahN suh dee-stree-bew-tuhr
The machine has eaten my card.	**Le distributeur a avalé ma carte.**
	luh dee-stree-bew-tuhr ah ah-vah-lay m̶ kahrt

FACT If you have an ATM, bank, or cre̶ card you should be able withdr̶ money from ATMs or cash machi̶ in French-speaking countries. If your PIN number is a word, make s̶ you memorize the number equivalents since many foreign ATMs do̶ have letters on their keypads. You'll probably have to pay service fee̶ both the card-issuing bank as well as the card's network (e.g., Cirr̶ Explore, Interlink, Plus, Star, etc.) for accessing the International A̶ System. Call your bank in advance to find out its international A̶ withdrawal fees. While you're on the phone, find out exactly how ma̶ digits your pin number can be in the country you're visiting; in Fra̶ ATMs usually accept four-digit pins only.

charge it

Can't figure out the currency exchange? Avoid the hassle and u̶ your credit card.

| Can I withdraw money on my credit card here? | **Est-ce que je peux retirer de l'arg̶ avec ma carte de crédit ici?** |
| | *ess kuh zhuh puh ruh-tee-ray duh lah-z̶ ah-vek mah kahrt duh kray-dee ee-see* |

Do you take credit cards?	**Vous acceptez les cartes de crédits?** *voo ahk-sep-tay lay kahrt duh kray-dee*
I'll pay by credit card.	**Je paie avec une carte de crédit.** *zhuh pay ah-vek ewn kahrt duh kray-dee*

You may be charged an international transaction fee—for each purchase made abroad—if you use a bank-issued credit card. Contact the credit card provider for info on fees.

pay up

Here's how to part with your hard-earned dough.

How much is it?	**Combien ça coûte?** *kohN-byaN sah koot*
Do you accept travelers checks?	**Acceptez-vous les chèques de voyage?** *ahk-sep-tay voo lay shek duh vwah-yahzh*
Could I have a receipt please?	**Est-ce que je peux avoir un ticket de caisse?** *ess kuh zhuh puh ah-vwah aN tee-keh duh kess*

The VAT—value-added tax (TVA in French)—you pay on purchases can be reclaimed when leaving France, Belgium, or Switzerland if you live outside the European Union. Get the refund forms from participating vendors, then have 'em stamped by a customs official at the airport.

4 HOTEL

get a room

You know you want to.

Can you recommend a hotel in …?

Pouvez-vous me recommander un hôtel à …?
poo-vay voo muh ruh-koh-mahN-day aN oh-tel ah

Is it near the center of town?

Est-ce près du centre-ville?
ess preh dew sahN-truh veel
You've gotta be close to the bars and clubs, right?!

How much is it per night?

Combien coûte une nuit?
kohN-byaN koot ewn nwee

Is there anything cheaper?

Y a-t-il quelque chose de moins cher?
ee ah-teel kel-kuh shohz duh mwaN shair

Could you reserve me a room there, please?

Pourriez-vous m'y réserver une chambre, s'il vous plaît?
poor-ee-ay voo mee ray-zair-vay ewn shahN-bruh seel voo pleh
If you're at the tourist information office, they may reserve the room for you.

I have a reservation.

J'ai réservé.
zhay ray-zair-vay

My name is …

Je m'appelle …
zhuh mah-pell

I confirmed by e-mail.

J'ai confirmé par e-mail.
zhay kohN-feer-may pahr e-mail

Could we have adjoining rooms?

Pourrions-nous avoir des chambres côte à côte?
poor-ee-ohN nooz ah-vwah day shahN-bruh koht ah koht

29

at the hotel

Need a room for tonight? Ask the right questions.

Do you have a room?	**Avez-vous des chambres libres?** *ah-vay voo day shahN-bruh lee-bruh*
I'd like …	**Je voudrais …** *zhuh voo-dray*
a single / double room.	**une chambre à un lit / chambre p deux personnes.** *ewn shahN-bruh ah aN lee / shahN-bru poor duh pair-sun*
a room with a bath / shower.	**une chambre avec salle de bains douche.** *ewn shahN-bruh ah-vek sahl duh baN /*

gotta have

Things you can't do without.

Does the hotel have …?	**Y a-t-il … à / dans l'hôtel?** *ee ah-teel … ah / dahN loh-tel*
cable TV	**la télévision par câble** *lah tay-lay-vee-zee-ohN pah kah-bluh*
internet access	**accès internet** *ahk-seh aN-tair-net*
a restaurant	**un restaurant** *aN res-toh-rahN*
room service	**un service de chambre** *aN sair-veess duh shahN-bruh*

a swimming pool	**une piscine**
	ewn pee-seen
a Wi-Fi® area	**un espace Wifi**
	aN es-pahss wee-fee
Is there … in the room?	**Y a-t-il … dans la chambre?**
	ee ah-teel … dahN lah shahN-bruh
air conditioning	**la climatisation**
	lah klee-mah-tee-zah-see-ohN
a phone	**le téléphone**
	luh tay-lay-fun
a TV	**la télévision**
	lah tay-lay-vee-zee-ohN

price

It all comes down to one thing.

How much is it …?	**Combien ça coûte …?**
	kohN-byaN sah koot
per night / week	**par nuit / semaine**
	pahr nwee / suh-men
Does the price include …?	**Est-ce-que cela comprend …?**
	ess kuh suh-lah cohN-prahN
breakfast	**le petit déjeuner**
	luh puh-tee day-zhuh-nay
sales tax [VAT]	**la T.V.A.**
	lah tay vay ah
Do I have to pay a deposit?	**Dois-je verser des arrhes?**
	dwah-zhuh vair-say days ahr

problems

Tell 'em what's bothering you.

I've lost my key. **J'ai perdu ma clé.**
zhay pair-dew mah klay

The lock is broken. **La serrure est cassée.**
lah sair-ewr eh kah-say

The … doesn't work. **… ne marche pas.**
nuh mahrsh pah

 fan **Le ventilateur**
luh vahN-tee-lah-tuhr

 heat **Le chauffage**
luh shoh-fahzh

 light **La lumière**
lah lewm-yair

There's no hot water / **Il n'y a pas d'eau chaude / de**
toilet paper. **papier toilette.**
eel nee ah pah doh shode / duh pah-pyay
twah-let

FACT Don't get burnt out. If you bring your own electrical gizmos to French-speaking Europe, you may need to buy an adapter (Continental adaptor plug—round pins, not square) to fit the various types of electrical sockets. You may also need a transformer appropriate to the wattage of the appliance. The 220-volt, 50-cycle AC is now almost universal in France, Belgium, and Switzerland, although 110 volts may still be encountered, especially in older buildings.

necessities

More importantly…

Where's the bar?

Où est le bar?
oo eh luh bah
This may be the most important
expression in the entire book.

Where's the swimming
pool?

Où est la piscine?
oo eh lah pee-seen

Where are the restrooms?

Où sont les toilettes?
oo sohN lay twah-let

What time is the front
door locked?

À quelle heure fermez-vous la
porte d'entrée?
ah kel-uhr fair-may voo lah pawrt dahN-tray
If you're staying at a guest
house, bed and breakfast, or even
a hostel, you may have a curfew!

What time is breakfast
served?

À quelle heure servez-vous le
petit déjeuner?
a kel uhr sair-vay voo luh puh-tee
day-zhuh-nay
If breakfast is included, don't
miss out!

Could you wake me
at … please?

Pourriez-vous me réveiller à …,
s'il vous plaît?
poor-ee-ay voo muh ray-vay-ay ah …
seel voo pleh

Can I leave this in the
hotel safe?

Puis-je laisser ceci dans le
coffre-fort de l'hôtel?
pwee-zhuh less-say suh-see dahN luh
kaw-fruh-fawr duh loh-tel

33

May I have an extra ...?	**Puis-je avoir ... supplémentaire?**
	pwee-zhuh ah-vwah ...
	sew-play-mahN-tair
bath towel	**une serviette de bain**
	ewn sair-vyett duh baN
blanket	**une couverture**
	ewn koo-vair-tewr
pillow	**un oreiller**
	aN noh-ray-ay
roll of toilet paper	**un rouleau de papier toilette**
	aN roo-loh duh pah-pyay twah-let
Are there any messages for me?	**Y a-t-il des messages pour moi?**
	ee ah-teel day mes-sahzh poor mwah
	Waiting for that special someone to call?

hostel

Looking for budget accommodations? The language you need is right here.

Do you have any places left for tonight?	**Vous reste-t-il des places pour ce soir?**
	voo rest-teel day plass poor suh swah
Do you rent bedding?	**Louez-vous des draps?**
	loo-ay voo day drah
What time are the doors locked?	**À quelle heure les portes ferment-elles?**
	ah kel uhr lay pawrt fairm-tell
I have an International Student Card.	**J'ai une carte d'étudiant internationale.**
	zhay ewn kart day-tew-dyahN aN-tair-nah-see-oh-nahl

the scoop

Hostels are a great way to get to know young travelers from Europe and elsewhere. France has more than 150 hostels nation-wide, Belgium has more than a dozen, Switzerland has about 60—just to name a few. If dormitory-style accommodations aren't for you, try booking in advance, online, or by phone. Though many hostels offer single and/or double rooms, they're usually reserved weeks ahead of time by savvy travelers who enjoy their privacy. Visit www.hiusa.org for more info.

check out

It's time to go.

What time do we have to check out?	**À quelle heure devons-nous libérer la chambre?** *ah kel uhr duh-vohN noo lee-bay-ray lah shahN-bruh*
May I have my bill, please?	**Puis-je avoir ma note, s'il vous plaît?** *pwee-zhuh ah-vwah mah nawt seel voo pleh*
I think there's a mistake in this bill.	**Je crois qu'il y a une erreur sur cette note.** *zhuh kwa keel ee ah ewn air-uhr sewr set nawt*
I've taken ... from the mini-bar.	**J'ai pris ... au mini-bar.** *zhay pree ... oh mee-nee bah* *You lush.*

camping

If camp is your thing, here's the info you need.

Is there a camp site nearby?	**Y a-t-il un camping près d'ici?** *ee ah-teel aN kahN-ping preh dee-see*
Do you have space for a tent?	**Avez-vous de la place pour une tente?** *ah-vay voo duh lah plahss poor ewn tahNt*
What is the charge per day / week?	**Quel est le tarif par jour / semaine?** *kel eh luh tah-reef pahr zhoor / suh-men*
Are there cooking facilities on site?	**Est-il possible de faire la cuisine sur le terrain?** *et-eel paws-see-bluh duh fair lah kwee-zeen sewr luh tair-aN*
Where are the showers?	**Où sont les douches?** *oo sohN lay doosh*

FACT

Camping in France is fun, easy, and inexpensive. A "camping municipal", public campsite, can be found in most towns; some tourist areas will also have privately owned campsites. If you're looking for a little rest and relaxation, try camping off-season at any one of France's many campsites on the beach, near lakes and rivers, or in the countryside.

where to eat

What are ya in the mood for?

Let's go to …	**On va …** *ohN vah*
a bistro.	**au bistro.** *oh bees-troh* *You'll find typical French fare here—not burgers and fries, but "steak frites", steak with fries.*
a buffet.	**au self.** *oh self* *Short for: "self-service".*
a cafe.	**au café.** *oh kah-fay*
a cafeteria.	**à la cafèt.** *ah lah kah-feht*
a diner.	**a diner.** *ah dee-nay*
a fast-food joint.	**au fast food.** *oh fast food*
a pizzeria.	**à la pizzeria.** *ah lah peed-zair-ee-ah*
a restaurant.	**au resto.** *oh res-toh* *The quick way to say, "au restaurant".*
a little eating place.	**au boui-boui.** *oh boo-ee-boo-ee* *Similar to a dive this tiny restaurant with less than appealing décor usually has pretty decent food.*

Now that you know where to eat, you'd better learn *when* to eat.

le petit déjeuner
luh puh-tee day-zhuh-nay
Grab breakfast anytime between 7–10 a.m. Order "un croissant" and "un petit noir", a small black coffee.

le déjeuner
luh day-zhuh-nay
Lunch is early: from 12–2 p.m. The French like to linger over a good meal so, if you don't have the time, opt for fast food or a baguette and cheese instead of restaurant fare.

le dîner
luh dee-nay
Be prepared to eat late—the French have dinner between 8–10 p.m.

 Take note. "Entrée" means appetizer, not main course. "Plat" is your main dish; "dessert" is… well, you know… dessert! The French eat a side salad after the main course, not before. And remember to drink your coffee after dessert, not during.

If you've got money to burn, try "haute cuisine", classic—and expensive—fine French food, or "nouvelle cuisine", modern meals prepared by celebrity chefs. Before you pick a restaurant, check out the menu, usually on display.

fast food

In a rush? Grab a quick bite to eat so you can keep sightseeing…

Is there a … restaurant nearby?	**Y a-t-il un restaurant … près d'ici?** *ee ah-teel aN res-toh-rahN … preh dee-see*
cheap	**bon marché** *bohN mah-shay*
French	**français** *frahN-say*
vegetarian	**végétarien** *vay-zhay-tah-ryaN*
Where can I find …?	**Où puis-je trouver …?** *oo pwee zhuh troo-vay*
a burger stand	**un kiosque à hamburger** *aN kee-osk ah ahm-buh-gair*
a café	**un café** *aN kah-fay*
a fast-food joint	**un fast-food** *aN fast food*
a pizzeria	**une pizzeria** *ewn peed-zair-ee-ah*
I'd like …	**Je voudrais …** *zhuh voo-dray*
a burger.	**un hamburger.** *aN ahm-buh-gair*
fries.	**des frites.** *day freet*
a pizza.	**une pizza.** *ewn peed-zah*
a sandwich.	**un sandwich.** *aN sahNd-weesh*

It's to go.	**C'est pour emporter.** *seh poor aN-paw-tay*
That's all, thanks.	**C'est tout, merci.** *seh too mair-see*
Enjoy your meal!	**Bon ap! / Bon appétit!** *bohN nahp / bohN nahp-puh-tee*

table manners

Go ahead, treat yourself. You deserve a meal at a swanky restaurant!

A table for two, please.	**Une table pour deux, s'il vous plaît.** *ewn tah-bluh poor duh seel voo pleh* *On a date?*
Could we sit …?	**Pouvons-nous nous asseoir …?** *poo-vohN noo noo zah-swah* *Find a cozy, romantic spot.*
outside	**dehors** *duh-awr*
in a non-smoking area	**dans une zone non-fumeur** *dahN zewn zon nohN few-muhr* *In France, you may have a problem finding a non-smoking area…*
by the window	**près de la fenêtre** *preh duh lah fuh-net-truh*
Where are the restrooms?	**Où sont les toilettes?** *oo sohN lay twah-let*
Waiter! / Waitress!	**Monsieur ♂! / Mademoiselle ♀!** *m'syewr / mahd-mwah-zel*

Could you tell me what … is?	**Pourriez-vous me dire ce qu'est …?**
	poor-yay voo muh deer suh keh
	Avoid the shock when your meal arrives…

| What's in it? | **Qu'y a-t-il dedans?** |
| | *kee ah-teel duh-dahN* |

Without …	**Sans …**
	sahN
	Just tell them the ingredient you hate!

May I have some …?	**Puis-je avoir …?**
	pwee zhuh ah-vwah
	Check out the dictionary in the back to fill in the blank.

I can't eat food containing …	**Je ne dois pas manger de plats contenant …**
	zhuh nuh dwah pah mahN-zhay duh plah kohN-tuh-nahN
	Just fill in the blank with what bothers you.

Do you have vegetarian meals?	**Avez-vous des plats végétariens?**
	ah-vay voo day plah vay-zhay-tar-yaN
	France isn't known for its vegetarian cuisine, but the chef may try to accommodate you. If not, stick to an omelet or meatless salad.

| I'm a vegan. | **Je suis végétalien ♂ / végétalienne ♀.** |
| | *zhuh swee vay-zhay-tahl-yaN / vay-zhay-tahl-yaNyen* |

complaints

Go ahead and make a big stink.

That's not what I ordered. **Ce n'est pas ce que j'ai commandé.**
suh neh pah suh kuh zhay kohN-mahN-day

I asked for … **J'ai demandé …**
zhay duh-mahN-day

The food is cold. **La nourriture est froide.**
lah noo-ree-tewr eh fwahd

This isn't clean. **Ce n'est pas propre.**
suh neh pah proh-pruh

How much longer will **Il y en a encore pour combien**
our food be? **de temps?**
eel yahN nah ahN-kaw poor kohN-byaN
duh tahN
You must be famished!

We can't wait any longer. **Nous ne pouvons plus attendre.**
We're leaving. **Nous partons.**
noo nuh poo-vohN plew ah-tahN-druh
noo pah-tohN

good or gross?

Give the chef a compliment—or not.

It's … **C'est …**
seh

delicious. **délicieux.**
day-lee-syuh

disgusting. **dégoûtant.**
day-goo-tahN

It's …	C'est …
	seh
foul.	**infect.**
	aN-fekt
(super) good.	**(super) bon.**
	(sew-pair) bohN
gross.	**dégueulasse.**
	day-guh-lahss
vile.	**infâme.**
	aN-fahm

pay up

How much did that meal set you back?

The check, please.	**L'addition, s'il vous plaît.**
	lah-dee-see-ohN seel voo pleh
We'd like to pay separately.	**Nous voudrions payer séparément.**
	noo voo-dree-ohn pay-ay say-pah-ray-mahN
	Goin' Dutch?
It's all together, please.	**Tous les repas ensemble, s'il vous plaît.**
	too lay ruh-pah ahN-sahN-bluh seel voo pleh
I think there's a mistake in this check.	**Je crois qu'il y a une erreur sur l'addition.**
	zhuh kwa keel ee ah ewn eh-ruhr sewr lah-dee-see-ohn
What is this amount for?	**Que représente ce montant?**
	kuh ruh-pray-zahNt suh mohN-tahN

I didn't have that. I had …	**Je n'ai pas pris ça. J'ai pris …**
	zhuh nay pah pree sah zhay pree
Is service included?	**Le service est-il compris?**
	luh sair-veess eh-teel kohN-pree
	Sometimes it is, sometimes it isn't—always best to ask.
Can I pay with this credit card?	**Puis-je payer avec cette carte de crédit?**
	pwee-zhuh pay-ay ah-vek set kahrt duh kray-dee
I've forgotten my wallet.	**J'ai oublié mon porte-monnaie.**
	zhay oo-blee-ay mohN pawrt mohN-nay
	Oh, god!
I don't have enough money.	**Je n'ai pas assez d'argent.**
	zhuh nay pah zah-say dah-zhahN
	Pretty embarrassing…
Could I have a receipt?	**Puis-je avoir un reçu?**
	pwee-zhuh ah-vwah aN ruh-sew

FACT

To tip or not to tip?

France: A 15% service fee is included in the check. It's customary, though, to round the check up 1-2 euros (€). If you've enjoyed a meal at an upscale spot, leave an extra 5%.

Belgium: The tip is included in the bill. No need to tip twice unless the service has been exceptional.

Switzerland: Even if your check is marked "service compris", service included, round up the check.

Quebec Province, Canada: Service usually isn't included in the check, so leave 15% of the total—before tax—for the wait staff.

breakfast

Whether you have it early or late, ask for…

I'd like (some) …	**Je voudrais …** *zhuh voo-dray*
bread.	**du pain.** *dew paN*
butter.	**du beurre.** *dew buhr*
eggs.	**des œufs.** *day zuh*
jam.	**de la confiture.** *duh lah kohN-fee-tewr*
juice.	**un jus.** *aN zhew*
milk.	**du lait.** *dew lay*
rolls.	**des petits pains.** *day puh-tee paN*
toast.	**du pain grillé.** *dew paN gree-yay*

soup's on

Homemade and delicious—here are the top picks.

garlic soup	**aïgo bouïdo** PROVENCE *ah-ee-goh bwee-doh*
seafood soup	**bouillabaisse** MARSEILLES *boo-yah-bess*
French onion soup	**soupe à l'oignon** *soup ah lohN-yohN*

And the good ol' standards…

… soup	**soupe …** *soup* *Also known as: bouillon, consommé, crème, potage, velouté.*
beer	**à la bière** *ah la bee-yair* *Only the French can make a soup out of beer!*
cabbage	**aux choux** *oh shoo*
chicken	**de volaille** *duh voh-ligh-yuh*
fish	**de poisson** *duh pwah-sohN*

 yo! Traveling around French-speaking Europe? Here are some snacks you've gotta try.

chocolat
shoh-koh-lah
Belgian chocolate may be the best in the world.

crêpe
krep
Grab this pancake from a street vendor.

frites
freet
Try French fries with mayo—Belgian-style.

quiche
keesh
This cheese and egg tart can include veggies or meat.

fish

The coastal areas of Belgium and France are well known for their fish and seafood. You've gotta try…

bar aux herbes en chemise
bahr oh-zairb ahN shuh-meez
It's bass stuffed with spinach and herbs, wrapped in lettuce and poached in white wine.

cotriade
koh-tree-yahd
A favorite of Brittany, France, this is a stew with shellfish, onion, carrots, potatoes, garlic, Calvados, and white wine.

homard à l'américaine
oh-mahr ah lah-may-ree-ken
Try this lobster, sautéed in cognac and then simmered in wine, aromatic vegetables, herbs, and tomatoes.

salade antiboise
salad ahN-tee-bwahz
This fish salad includes cooked diced fish, anchovy fillets, green peppers, beets, rice, and capers in dressing.

Or stick with your favorites…

cod	**morue** *moh-rew*
crab	**crabe** *crahb*
mackerel	**maquereau** *mahk-roh*
mussels	**moules** *mool*

oysters	**huîtres** *weet-ruh*
salmon	**saumon** *so-mohN*
snails	**escargots** *es-kah-goh*
sole	**sole** *sull*
tuna	**thon** *tohN*
trout	**truite** *trweet*

you carnivore

France is a meat-eater's dream come true. Here are the must haves.

blanquette de veau
blahN-ket duh voh
veal stew in a white sauce, with onions and mushrooms

bœuf bourguignon
buhf boor-geen-yohN
a hearty beef stew with vegetables and a hint of red wine

coq au vin
kawk oh vaN
chicken with onion, mushroom, and bacon in wine sauce

ragoût
rah-goo
meat stew, generally served in a delicate gravy with veggies

Not sure what to order? Stick with the basics.

I'd like some …   **Je voudrais …**
                         zhuh voo-dray

bacon.   **du lard.**
                         dew lahr

beef.   **du bœuf.**
                         dew buhf

chicken.   **du poulet.**
                         dew poo-leh

ham.   **du jambon.**
                         dew zhahN-bohN

lamb.   **de l'agneau.**
                         duh lahn-yoh

pork.   **du porc.**
                         dew pawr

sausage.   **des saucisses.**
                         day soh-seess

steak.   **du steak.**
                         dew stek

veal.   **du veau.**
                         dew voh

herbivore

For something a little lighter, try these favorites.

green salad   **salade verte**
                         sah-lahd vairt

tossed salad   **salade composée**
                         sah-lahd kohN-poh-zay

tuna salad	**salade niçoise** *sah-lahd nee-swahz* *Try this salad with tuna, anchovies, olives, and vegetables.*
veggie salad	**salade russe** *sah-lahd rewss* *It's potatoes, carrots, peas, hard-boiled eggs in mayo.*

Your basic veggies…

artichoke	**artichaut** *ah-tee-shoh*
carrots	**carottes** *kah-rawt*
cucumber	**concombre** *kohN-kohN-bruh*
green beans	**haricots verts** *ah-ree-koh vair*
lettuce	**laitue** *lay-tew*
mushrooms	**champignons** *shahN-peen-yohN*
onions	**oignons** *ohN-yohN*
peas	**petits pois** *puh-tee pwah*
potatoes	**pommes (de terre)** *pum (duh tair)*
tomatoes	**tomates** *toh-maht*

cheese please

France has an amazing selection of local cheese—there are more than 400 varieties! Try…

mild cheese	**beaumont, belle étoile, boursin, brie, cantal, coulommiers, mimolette, Port-Salut, reblochon, saint-paulin, tomme**
sharp, tangy cheese	**bleu de Bresse, brousse, camembert, livarot, maroilles, munster, pont-l'évêque, roquefort, vacherin**
goat's milk	**bûcheron, cabécou, crottin de Chavignol, fromage de chèvre, rocamadour, st-marcellin, valençay**
Swiss cheese	**beaufort, comté, emmental, gruyère**

dessert

End your meal with any one of these delicious sweets.

diplomate
dee-ploh-maht
It's a molded custard dessert with crystallized fruit and lined with sponge cake fingers steeped in strong liqueur.

glace
glahss
France is known for its fresh ice cream; some common flavors are: "à la vanille", vanilla; "au chocolat", chocolate; "à la fraise", strawberry.

mousse au chocolat
moos oh shoh-koh-lah
Who can resist chocolate mousse?

profiteroles
proh-fee-tair-awl
They're the most amazing cream puffs that you'll ever taste. Melted dark chocolate on top makes them decadent!

soufflé au chocolat
soo-flay oh shoh-koh-lah
Chocolate souffle, anyone?

tarte Tatin
taht tah-taN
It's hot caramelized apples, topped with pastry, and served with vanilla ice cream or "crème anglaise", custard.

overeating

Did you just pig out?

I'm full.	**Je cale.** *zhuh kahl*
I ate too much.	**J'ai trop mangé.** *zhay troh mahN-zhay*
I'm overstuffed.	**J'ai les dents du fond qui baignent.** *zhay lay dahN dew fohN kee ben-yuh* *Literally: My molars are soaking.*

what to drink

When you need to detox, ask for…

I'd like a …

Je voudrais …
zhuh voo-dray

(hot) chocolate.

un chocolat (chaud).
aN shoh-koh-lah (shoh)

coke.

un coca.
aN koh-kah

juice.

un jus.
aN zhew

apple

de pomme
duh pum

grapefruit

de pamplemousse
duh pahM-pluh-moos

orange

d'orange
doh-rahNzh

mineral water.

de l'eau minérale.
duh loh mee-nay-rahl

carbonated

gazeuse
gah-zuhz

non-carbonated

non gazeuse
nohN gah-zuhz

the scoop

Just about everybody in France drinks mineral water. Favorites are: Badoit®, Evian®, Perrier®, Vichy®, Vittel®, Volvic®. Order by brand at your favorite little café or bar! If you don't wanna spend your cash on water, ask for "une carafe d'eau", a pitcher of tap water.

coffee culture

Get your daily dose of caffeine.

I'd like a cup of tea / coffee.	**Je voudrais une tasse de thé / café.** *zhuh voo-dray ewn tahss duh tay / kah-fay*
A black coffee.	**Un café noir.** *aN kah-fay nwah*
An espresso.	**Un espresso.** *aN es-press-oh*
Coffee with milk, please.	**Un café au lait, s'il vous plaît.** *aN kah-fay oh lay seel voo pleh*

the Scoop

You haven't been to Paris until if you've experienced café life. Sit outside and people-watch as you sip your "café au lait", coffee with milk; "décaféiné" or "déca", decaffeinated coffee; "frappé", shaken, iced coffee. Most young Parisians simply order "un café", coffee (black and strong, served in a small cup), since it's half the price of a fancy coffee beverage.

Though it's less popular, you can also order "un thé", tea. Most French guys and girls drink tea "au citron", with lemon; "à la menthe", mint; "glacé", iced; or "nature", black, but you can also order it "au lait", with milk. Try "tisane", herbal tea; it's a popular non-caffeine alternative that comes in a variety of flavors.

beer

eady for a buzz?

you have … beer?	**Avez-vous de la bière …?** *ah-vay voo duh lah bee-yair*

bottled	**en bouteille** *aN boo-tay*
draft	**en pression** *ahN press-yohN*

… beer, please.	**Une bière …, s'il vous plaît.** *ewn bee-yair … seel voo pleh*

light	**blonde** *blohNd* *This is a light, Pilsner-style beer,* *e.g., Jupiler, Lamot, Stella Artois.*
red	**brune** *brewn* *Refreshing but with a sour* *kick, e.g., Rodenbach.*
white	**blanche** *blahNsh* *It's cloudy and honeyish; try* *Hoegaarden or Kwak.*

Go Belgian if you want to sample the king of beer. There are hundreds of varieties—more than 400—and each has its own unique beer glass, complete with the brand's label. That makes t easy to order the local brew!

57

drink up

There's no faster way to get a party started.

Do you want …?
Tu veux …?
tew vuh

an aperitif
un apéro
aN ah-pair-oh
It's the short form of "apéritif"

wine
du pinard
dew pee-nahr
Literally: cheap wine

a glass of red wine
un coup de rouge
aN coo-duh roozh
Literally: a shot of red

a shot
un verre
aN vair
How about "un rhum", "une vodka", "un whisky" (but not a three simultaneously)?

a gin and tonic
un gin tonic
aN zheen toh-neek

a screwdriver
une vodka orange
ewn vohd-kah oh-rahNzh

 To tip or not to tip?

Belgium, France, Switzerland: Leaving a tip for the bartender is up to you Most patrons leave a euro or two (2–3 francs if you're in Switzerland).

Quebec Province, Canada: Tip your bartender generously, 10–15%, and you'll get great service and perhaps even a free round.

wino

Go ahead and order a glass—or bottle—of the best.

May I see the wine list, please?	**Puis-je avoir la carte des vins, s'il vous plaît?**
	pwee-zhuh ah-vwah lah kahrt day vaN seel voo pleh
	"Le sommelier", the wine waiter, will be happy to offer advice—for a tip, of course.
Can you recommend a wine?	**Pouvez-vous nous recommander un vin?**
	poo-vay voo noo ruh-kohN-mahN-day aN vaN
I'd like … of …	**Je voudrais … de …**
	zhuh voo-dray … duh
a bottle	**une bouteille**
	ewn boo-tay
a carafe	**une carafe**
	ewn kah-rahf
a glass	**un verre**
	aN vair

Make friends at a bar.

– **Je t'offre un verre?**
zhuh tawf-fruh aN vair
Can I buy you a drink?

– **OK, pourquoi pas.**
oh-keh poor-kwah pah
Sure, why not.

59

cheers

Before you drink, make a toast.

Let's celebrate!   **Ça s'arrose!**
sah-sah-rawz
Literally: Let's sprinkle!

Let's cheer!   **Trinquons!**
traN-kohN

Cheers!   **À la tienne!**
ah lah tee-yen
Literally: To yours!

the scoop

There's nothing like a good ol' French bubbly. The Champagne region is just an hour ride from Paris, so there's every reason to sample the drink right at the vineyard. Follow "La Route Touristique du Champagne", the tourist's route of Champagne, to get info from the source—and enjoy tastings, of course. Wherever you decide to enjoy your bubbly be sure to...

■ Open the bottle gently: remove the foil, the wire cage, and hold the cork as you slowly turn the bottle.

■ Drink it chilled, but never iced.

■ Use a Champagne flute, which allows bubbles to move freely.

■ Finish the bottle in one sitting!

hangover

Drank too much? Not feeling too well?
Share your discomfort.

like to drink.

J'aime picoler.
zhem pee-caw-lay

m tipsy!

Je suis pompette!
zhuh swee pum-pet

ve had one drink too many.

J'ai un verre dans le nez.
zhay aN vair dahN luh neh
Literally: I have one drink in
the nose.

m hung over.

J'ai la gueule de bois.
zhay lah guhl duh bwah
Literally: I have a wooden head.

m hung over.

J'ai mal aux cheveux.
zhay mahl oh shuh-vuh
Literally: My hair hurts.

FACT

The drinking age in France is 18, but it certainly isn't enforced. You might see teenagers hanging out at cafés nd drinking beer, and no one is shocked. Minors can easily purchase lcohol. Perhaps because drinking isn't seen as a big deal, the French on't even have an expression for "binge drinking"!

beach bum

Grab your shades and get some sun.

Is it a nude beach?

Est-ce une plage nudiste?
ess ewn plahzh new-deest

Is there a swimming pool here?

Y a-t-il une piscine ici?
ee ah-teel ewn pee-seen ee-see

Is it safe to swim / dive here?

Est-ce qu'on peut se baigner / plonger ici sans danger?
ess kohN puh suh bain-yay / plohN-zhay ee-see sahN dahN-zhay

Is there a lifeguard?

Y a-t-il un maître-nageur?
ee ah-teel aN meh-truh nah-zhuhr
What you really want to know is: Is the lifeguard hot?!

I want to rent …

Je voudrais louer …
zhuh voo-dray loo-ay

a deck chair.

une chaise longue.
ewn shehz lohNg

a jet ski.

un scooter de mer.
aN skoo-tuhr duh mehr

a motorboat.

un canot automobile.
aN kah-noh oh-toh-moh-beel

a surfboard.

une planche de surf.
ewn plahNsh duh suhrf

an umbrella.

un parasol.
aN pah-rah-sawl

waterskis.

des skis nautiques.
day skee noh-teek

63

the scoop

France's Côte d'Azur is the place to see and be seen. Whether you're laying on the sand in front of the luxury hotels or watching the beautiful jet set walk along the promenades, keep your eyes open for the rich and famous. The French Riviera is the summertime playground of famed clothing designers, popular actors, favorite musicians… the A-list just keeps on goin'!

party time

Parisians know how to have a good time.

What's there to do at night?	**Qu'est-ce qu'il y a à faire le soir?** *kess keel yah ah fair luh swah*
Let's hang out tonight.	**On sort ce soir.** *ohN sawr suh swah*
Let's go to …	**On se fait …** *ohN suh feh*
the movies.	**un ciné / une toile.** *aN see-nay / ewn twahl*
the theater.	**une pièce de théâtre.** *ewn pee-ess duh tay-ah-truh*
a concert.	**un concert.** *aN kohN-sair*

Can you recommend a …?	**Pouvez-vous me recommander un ♂ / une ♀ …?**
	poo-vay voo muh ruh-kohN-mahN-day aN /ewn
Is there … in town?	**Est-ce qu'il y a … en ville?**
	ess keel yah … ahN veel
a bar	**un bar**
	aN bah
a casino	**un casino**
	aN kah-zee-noh
a dance club	**une discothèque / une boîte (de nuit)**
	ewn dees-koh-tek / ewn bwaht (duh nwee)
a gay club	**un club gay**
	aN kluhb gay
a nightclub	**un night-club**
	aN night-kluhb
What type of music do they play?	**Quel genre de musique jouent-ils?**
	kel zhahN-ruh duh mew-zeek zhoo-teel
How do I get there?	**Comment est-ce que je peux m'y rendre?**
	kohN-mohN ess-kuh zhuh puh mee rahN-druh

smoke

Whether you'd like to light up or want to share your distaste of smoking with those around you, here's the language you need.

| Do you smoke? | **Tu fumes?** |
| | *tew fewm* |

65

Want to have a smoke?	**On s'en grille une?**
	ohN sahN gree ewn
	Literally: Do you want to grate one?

	Tu as …?
	tew ah
	une clope
	ewn klawp
Do you have a <u>cigarette</u>?	**une garo**
	ewn gah-roh
	une nuigrav
	ewn nwee-grahv
	From, "nuit gravement à la santé,"
	very dangerous for your health, the
	warning label on a pack of cigarettes.

For those who know smoking is a nasty habit.

– Tu fumes?
tew fewm
Do you smoke?

_____

– Non!
nohN
No!

the
SCOOP

You'll find few smoke-free areas in France—smoking restrictions apply mainly to healthcare facilities, schools, offices, buses, and taxis—and smoking is allowed and accepted almost everywhere. Law requires restaurants and bars to have a smoking and a non-smoking section, but it's rarely enforced.

spa

You need complete relaxation.

I'd like …
Je voudrais …
zhuh voo-dray

a facial.
un nettoyage de peau.
aN net-twah-yahzh duh poh

a manicure.
une manucure.
ewn mahn-ew-kewr

a massage.
un massage.
aN mah-sahzh

a pedicure.
une pédicure / un soin des pieds.
ewn pay-dee-kewr / aN swaN day pyay

a bikini wax.
une épilation du maillot.
ewn ay-pee-lah-see-ohN dew my-yoh

an eyebrow wax.
une épilation des sourcils.
ewn ay-pee-lah-see-ohN day soor-see

body alterations

Blend in with the locals.

Did you have plastic surgery?
Tu as fait de la chirurgie esthétique?
tew ah feh duh lah sheer-ewr-zhee es-tay-teek

I had …
Je me suis fait refaire …
zhuh muh swee feh ruh-fair

a boob job.
les seins.
lay saN

a nose job.
le nez.
luh nay

a tummy tuck.
le ventre.
luh vahN-truh

I had my lips enhanced.	**Je me suis fait gonfler les lèvres.**
	zhuh muh swee feh gohN-flay lay lehv-ruh
He / She got a tattoo.	**Il / Elle s'est fait tatouer.**
	eel / el seh feh tah-too-ay
He / She has a / an … piercing.	**Il / Elle a un piercing au …**
	eel / el ah aN peer-sing oh
belly button	**nombril.**
	nohN-breel
eyebrow	**sourcil.**
	soor-see
nipple	**téton.**
	tay-tohN
nose	**nez.**
	nay

the sights

Now that you're looking good, see and be seen.

Where's the tourist information office?	**Où est l'office du tourisme?**
	oo eh lawf-eess dew toor-eez-muh
Can you recommend a sightseeing tour?	**Pouvez-vous recommander une visite touristique?**
	poo-vay voo ruh-kohN-mahN-day ewn veezeet tooreesteek
	A great way to meet other cute travelers, like yourself!
Are there any trips to …?	**Y a-t-il des voyages à …?**
	ee ah-teel day vwah-yahzh ah
	There are a million ways you can end this question while in Paris. Some suggestions: Versailles, Sèvres, Chantilly, Fontainebleau…

| What time does the tour start? | **À quelle heure commence l'excursion?** |
| | *ah kel uhr kohN-mahNs lex-kewr-see-ohN* |

| How much does the tour cost? | **Combien coûte cette excursion?** |
| | *kohN-bayN koot set ex-kewr-see-ohN* |

| What time do we get back? | **À quelle heure revenons-nous?** |
| | *ah kel uhr ruh-vuh-nohN noo* |

| Is there an English-speaking guide? | **Y a-t-il un ♂ / une ♀ guide qui parle anglais?** |
| | *ee ah-teel aN / ewn gheed kee pahl ahN-gleh* |

| Can we stop here …? | **Est-ce que nous pouvons nous arrêter ici …?** |
| | *ess kuh noo poo-vohN noo zah-ret-tay ee-see* |

| to buy souvenirs | **pour acheter des souvenirs** |
| | *poor ahsh-tay day soo-veh-neer* |

| to use the restrooms | **pour aller aux toilettes** |
| | *poor ah-lay oh twah-let* |

to take photographs	**pour prendre des photos**
	poor prahN-druh day foh-toh
	Capture the memory.

Would you take a photo of us?	**Pourriez-vous nous prendre en photo?**
	poor-yay voo noo prahN-druh aN foh-toh
	Ask a cute French guy or girl!

| Where is …? | **Où est …?** |
| | *oo eh* |

| the art gallery | **la galerie d'art** |
| | *lah gahl-ree dahr* |

| the botanical garden | **le jardin botanique** |
| | *luh zhahr-daN boh-tah-neek* |

Where is …?	**Où est …?**
	oo eh
the castle	**le château**
	luh shah-toh
the cemetery	**le cimetière**
	luh seem-tyair
the church	**l'église**
	lay-gleez
the downtown area	**le centre ville**
	luh sahN-truh veel
the market	**le marché**
	luh mahr-shay
the (war) memorial	**le monument (aux morts)**
	luh mohN-new-mahN (oh mawr)
the museum	**le musée**
	luh mew-zay
the old town	**la vieille ville**
	lah vyay veel
the palace	**le palais**
	luh pah-leh
the shopping area	**les rues commerçantes**
	lay rew kum-mair-sahNt
the tower	**la tour**
	lah toor
the town hall	**l'hôtel de ville**
	loh-tel duh veel
How much is the entrance fee?	**Combien coûte l'entrée?**
	kohN-byaN koot lahN-tray
Are there any discounts for students?	**Y a-t-il des réductions pour les étudiants?**
	ee ah-teel day ray-dewk-see-ohN poor lay zay-tew-dyahN

the scoop

Did you see something totally cool? Here are the top ten ways to say it.

Cool!	**Cool!** *kooool* *Say it with a "cool" French accent, of course.*
Very cool!	**Tip-top!** *teep-tawp*
Great!	**Géant!** *zhay-ahN* *Literally: Giant!*
Great!	**D'enfer!** *dahN-fair* *Literally: From hell!*
Killer!	**C'est de la mort qui tue!** *seh duh lah mawr kee tew* *Literally: It's deadly killing!*
Nice!	**Sympa!** *saN-pah*
Perfect!	**Pile-poil!** *peel-pwahl*
Super!	**Super!** *soo-pehr*
Super!	**Extra!** *ex-trah*
Sweet! / Brilliant!	**Génial!** *zhay-nyahl* *Literally: Genius!*

71

entertainment

In the mood for a little culture?

Do you have a program of events?	**Avez-vous un programme des spectacles?** *ah-vay voo aN proh-grahm day spek-tahk-luh*
Can you recommend a good ...?	**Pouvez-vous me conseiller ...?** *poo-vay voo muh kohN-say-yay*
concert	**un concert** *aN kohN-sair*
movie	**un film** *aN feelm*
When does it start?	**À quelle heure est-ce que ça commence?** *ah kel uhr ess kuh sah kohM-mahNss*
Where can I get tickets?	**Où est-ce que je peux me procurer des billets?** *oo ess kuh zhuh puh muh proh-kewr-ay day bee-yay*
How much are the seats?	**Combien coûtent les places?** *kohN-byaN koot lay plahss*
Do you have anything cheaper?	**Avez-vous quelque chose de moins cher?** *ah-vay voo kel-kuh shohz duh mwaN shair*
Can I have a program?	**Est-ce que je peux avoir un programme?** *ess kuh zhuh puh ah-vwah aN proh-grahm*

movies

Behind-the-scenes movie lingo…

My favorite movies are … **Mes films préférés sont …**
may feelm pray-fair-ay sohN

comedies. **les comédies.**
lay cawm-ay-dee

dramas. **les drames psychologiques.**
lay drahm see-koh-loh-zheek

foreign films. **les films étrangers.**
lay feelm ay-trahN-zhay

thrillers. **les thrillers.**
lay threel-lair
You can also say, "les films noirs".

psycho-thrillers. **les psycho-thrillers.**
lay see-koh-threel-lair

What's playing at the movies? **Qu'y a-t-il au cinéma ce soir?**
kee ah-teel oh see-nay-mah suh swah

Is the movie dubbed / subtitled? **Est-ce que le film est doublé / sous-titré?**
ess kuh luh feelm eh doo-blay / soo-tee-tray

 Ever heard of "Festival de Cannes", the Cannes Film Festival? This annual international film festival is the place to be if you're in the movie industry. Tickets aren't available to the general public—it's by invitation only.

music

Get into the groove—French style.

Do you like …?	**Tu aimes …?**
	tew em
dance music	**la dance**
	lah dahnss
hip-hop	**le hip hop**
	luh eep-awp
house (music)	**la house**
	lah owss
jazz	**le jazz**
	luh dzhaz
pop (music)	**la pop**
	lah pawp
rap	**le rap**
	luh rahp
reggae	**le reggae**
	luh reh-geh
rock and roll	**le rock**
	luh rawk
techno	**la techno**
	lah tek-noh
I really like …	**J'aime beaucoup …**
	zhem boh-koo
country.	**la musique country.**
	lah mew-zeek kun-tree
folk.	**lah musique folk.**
	lah mew-zeek folk

soul. **la musique soul.**
lah mew-zeek sul

Which band is playing? **Quel groupe joue?**
kel groop zhoo

Are they popular? **Est-ce qu'ils sont connus?**
ess keel sohN kun-new

---

yo! Can't live without your tunes? Make sure you have these.

a CD player **un lecteur de CD**
an lek-tuhr duh say-day

a discman **un discman**
aN deesk-mahn

an MP3 player **un lecteur MP3**
aN lek-tuhr em-pay-twah

an iPod™ **un iPod™**
aN ee-pud

earphones **des écouteurs**
day zek-koo-tuhr

a stereo **une chaîne**
ewn shen

8 SPORTS & GAMBLING

sports

Get active.

| Do you want to try …? | **Tu veux essayer …?** |
| | *tew vuh es-ay-yay* |

French boxing	**la boxe française**
	lah bawx frahN-sez
	In French boxing, you use your feet to kick in addition to punching with your hands. Intense!

| karate | **le karaté** |
| | *luh kah-rah-tay* |

| spinning | **le vélo sur piste** |
| | *luh vay-loh sewr peest* |

| tai chi | **le tai chi chuan** |
| | *luh tie-chee-chwahn* |

| yoga | **le yoga** |
| | *luh yoh-gah* |

| I … | **Je fais …** |
| | *zhuh feh* |

| cycle. | **du vélo.** |
| | *dew vay-loh* |

| jog. | **du jogging.** |
| | *dew jawg-ging* |

| rollerblade. | **du roller.** |
| | *dew roh-lair* |

| skateboard. | **du skate.** |
| | *dew skate* |

| surf. | **du surf.** |
| | *dew suhrf* |

| swim. | **de la natation.** |
| | *duh lah nah-tah-see-ohN* |

Do you want to play …?	**Tu veux jouer au …?**
	tew vuh zjoo-ay oh
basketball	**basket**
	bahss-ket
soccer	**football**
	fuht-bawl
tennis	**tennis**
	ten-neess
volleyball	**volley**
	voh-lay

extreme sports

Take your game to the next level.

I want to go …	**Je veux faire …**
	zhuh vuh fair
skydiving.	**du saut en parachute.**
	dew soht ahN pah-rah-shewt
kayaking.	**du kayak.**
	dew kah-yahk
mountain-climbing.	**de l'alpinisme.**
	duh lahl-peen-eez-muh
rafting.	**du rafting.**
	dew rahf-ting
bungee jumping.	**du saut à l'élastique.**
	dew soht ah lay-lahss-teek

spectator sports

Prefer watching sports to actually playing them?

Is there a soccer game this Saturday?	**Y a-t-il un match de football samedi?** *ee ah-teel aN mahtch duh fuht-bawl sahm-dee*
Which teams are playing?	**Quelles sont les équipes?** *kel sohN lay zay-keep*
Can you get me a ticket?	**Pouvez-vous me procurer un ticket?** *poo-vay voo muh proh-kew-ray aN tee-kay*
What's the admission charge?	**Combien coûtent les places?** *kohN-byaN koot lay plahss*

soccer match

Show that you're true sports fans by screaming these.

Go!	**Allez!** *ah-lay*
Let's go!	**On y va!** *ohN ee vah*
Get them!	**Bouffez-les! / Explosez-les!** *boof-ay lay / ex-ploh-say-lay* *Literally: Eat them! / Explode them!*
Goal!	**But!** *bewt*
We're the champions!	**On est les champions!** *ohN eh lay shahN-pee-ohN*

insults

Don't forget that harassing the referee, "l'arbitre", and humiliating the opponent, "l'adversaire", is part of your job as a spectator.

The referee took a bribe!	**Vendu, l'arbitre!**
	vahN-dew lah-bee-truh
	Literally: Paid for!
Kick him out!	**Retourne au vestiaire! / Aux chiottes!**
	ruh-toorn oh ves-tyair / oh she-yawt
	Literally: Go to the locker room! / In the bathroom!
So predictable!	**Téléphoné!**
	tay-lay-fun-ay
	Literally: Telephoned!
You suck!	**Va te coucher / rhabiller!**
	vah tuh koo-shay / rah-bee-yay
	Literally: Go to bed / get dressed!
He sucks!	**Quel nul!**
	kel newl
	Literally: What a zero!
@#&! this player!	**Quel enculé / Quel merde, ce joueur!**
	kel ahN-kew-lay / kel maird suh zhoo-uhr

training

Don't let your body go just because you're on vacation.

Can I use …?	**Je peux utiliser …?**
	zhuh puh ew-tee-lee-zay
the fitness bike	**le vélo de salle**
	luh vay-loh duh sahl

the rowing machine	**le rameur**
	luh rah-muhr
the treadmill	**le tapis de course**
	luh tah-pee duh kurss

I feel great.	**J'ai la pêche.**
	zhay lah pesh
	Literally: I have the peach.

| I'm in shape. | **Je suis en forme.** |
| | *zhuh swee zahN fawrm* |

| I'm dead tired. | **Je suis mort♂ / morte♀.** |
| | *zhuh swee mawr / mawrt* |

| I can't take it anymore. | **J'en peux plus.** |
| | *zhahN puh plew* |

I'm sick of it.	**J'en ai plein le dos / le cul.**
	zhahN nay plaN luh doh / luh kew
	Literally: I have my back / ass full.

gambling

Got money to burn?

| Where's the racetrack? | **Où est l'hippodrome?** |
| | *oo eh leep-oh-drawm* |

| Is there a casino in town? | **Est-ce qu'il y a un casino en ville?** |
| | *ess keel yah aN kah-zee-noh ahN veel* |

| Do you want to …? | **Tu veux …?** |
| | *tew vuh* |

| bet | **parier** |
| | *pahr-yay* |

| bid | **miser** |
| | *mee-zay* |

Do you want to …?	**Tu veux …?**
	tew vuh
put all your money down	**risquer le paquet**
	rees-kay luh pah-keh
flip a coin	**jouer à pile ou face**
	zhoo-ay ah peel oo fahss
Do you want to play …?	**Tu veux jouer …?**
	tew vuh zhoo-ay
cards	**aux cartes**
	oh kahrt
gin	**au rami**
	oh rah-mee
poker	**au poker**
	oh poh-kair

poker face

Take control of the card game.

I have the deal.	**J'ai la main.** *zhay lah maN* *Literally: I have the hand.*
Do you want to cut [the deck]?	**Tu veux couper?** *tew vuh koo-pay*
I fold.	**Je me couche.** *zhuh muh koosh* *Literally: I'm going to sleep.*
Did you …?	**Tu as …?** *tew ah*
gamble it away	**perdu au jeu** *pair-dew oh juh*
lose it all	**tout perdu** *too pair-dew*
win the hand	**remporté la mise** *rahN-paw-tay lah meez*

Monte Carlo is a hotspot for upscale gamblers—the trendiest table games are on offer: American and European roulette; blackjack; poker; "chemin de fer", a game similar to baccarat; and more. If table games aren't your thing, there are more than 1000 slot machines and tons of video poker terminals where you can test your luck. You've gotta be 18 or older to play and must wear "suitable attire" (i.e., don't show up in your bikini and cut-off shorts) to enter.

small talk

Get a conversation goin'.

My name is …

Je m'appelle …
zhuh mah-pell
A simple way to introduce yourself.

What's your name?

Comment tu t'appelles?
kohN-mahN tew tah-pell

Where are you from?

D'où viens-tu?
doo vyaN tew

Whom are you with?

Avec qui es-tu?
ah-vek kee eh-tew

I'm on my own.

Je suis tout seul ♂ / toute seule ♀.
zhuh swee too suhl / toot suhl

I'm with a friend.

Je suis avec un ami ♂ / une amie ♀.
zhuh swee zah-vek aN ah-mee / ewn ah-mee
Oh, really?!

I'm with my …

Je suis avec …
zhuh swee zah-vek

boyfriend / girlfriend.

mon copain ♂ / ma copine ♀.
mohN koh-paN / mah koh-peen

family.

ma famille.
mah fah-mee-yuh

parents.

mes parents.
may pah-rahN

father / mother.

mon père ♂ / ma mère ♀.
mohN pair / mah mair

brother / sister.

mon frère ♂ / ma sœur ♀.
mohN frehr / mah suhr

85

chitchat

These will help you keep his or her attention.

What do you do? **Que fais-tu?**
kuh feh tew

What are you studying? **Tu étudies quoi?**
tew ay-tew-dee kwah

I'm studying ... **J'étudie ...**
zhay-tew-dee

the arts. **l'art.**
lahr

business. **le commerce.**
luh kum-airss

engineering. **l'ingénierie.**
laN-zhayn-yair-ee

sales. **la vente.**
la vahNt

science. **les sciences.**
lay see-ahNss

Whom do you work for?	**Pour qui travailles-tu?**
	poor kee trah-vah-yuh-tew

I work for …	**Je travaille pour …**
	zhuh trah-vah-yuh poor

What are your interests / hobbies?	**Quels sont tes intérêts / hobbies?**
	kel sohN tay zaN-tay-reh / awb-bee

makin' plans

Get together.

Are you free tonight?	**Est-ce que tu es libre ce soir?**
	ess kuh tew eh lee-bruh suh swah

Can you come for a drink this evening?	**Est-ce que tu peux venir prendre un verre ce soir?**
	ess kuh tew puh vuh-neer prahN-druh aN vair suh swah

Would you like to …?	**Est-ce que tu aimerais …?**
	ess kuh tew em-ray

go dancing	**aller danser**
	ah-lay dahN-say

go out to eat	**aller manger**
	ah-lay mahN-zhay

go for a walk	**faire une promenade**
	fair ewn prawm-nahd

Can I bring a friend?	**Est-ce que je peux amener un ami♂ / une amie♀?**
	ess kuh zhuh puh ahm-nay aN ah-mee / ewn ah-mee

Where should we meet?	**Où nous retrouvons-nous?**
	oo noo ruh-troo-vohN noo

hangin' out

Get a little closer with these.

Let me buy you a drink.
Permets-moi de t'offrir quelque chose à boire.
pair-meh-mwa duh toff-reer kel-kuh shot ah bwahr

What are you going to have?
Qu'est-ce que tu prends?
kess kuh tew prahN

Why are you laughing?
Pourquoi ris-tu?
poor-kwa ree tew

Is my French that bad?
Est-ce que mon français est si mauvais que ça?
ess kuh mohN frahN-seh eh see moh-veh kuh sah

Should we go somewhere quieter?
Si on allait dans un endroit un peu plus calme?
see ohN ah-lay dahN zaN nahN-drwah al puh plew kalm
Such as...?

Thanks for the evening.
Merci pour cette soirée.
mair-see poor set swah-ray

the scoop

Don't be cheap on a date; if you ask someone out, it's up to you to pay the bill. The French don't tend to "go Dutch" in restaurants. The person who has invited usually pays—with the other offering to return the favor next time.

get a date

Looking to score? Try these.

Hi, how are you?
Salut, ça va?
sah-lew sah vah
*It's simple—but a good way to
break the ice.*

Hello, I don't think
we've met.
**Bonjour, nous ne nous connaissons
pas, je crois?**
*bohN-zhoor noo nuh noo kohN-neh-sohN
pah zhuh kwah*
*If it's is your first visit to this
French-speaking country, it's
certainly the truth!*

Would you like to sit down?
Voulez-vous vous asseoir?
voo-lay-voo voo zah-swah
*This works wonders in a bar or
on the "Métro", subway.*

You are really sexy.
T'es trop sexy.
tay troh sex-ee
*The perfect informal come-on to
use in a bar or club.*

Are you a model?
Vous êtes mannequin?
voo zet mahn-neh-kaN
*You'd be surprised how well this
one works.*

You look great!
Tu es très beau ♂ / belle ♀ !
tew eh treh boh / bell

Do you mind if I sit here?
Ça vous dérange si je m'asseois ici?
*sah voo day-rahNzh see zhuh mah-swah
ee-see*

refusals

Not your type? Here are the best ways to reject someone.

Thanks, but I'm expecting someone.	**Merci, mais j'attends quelqu'un.**
	mair-see meh zhah-tahN kel-kaN
	Whether this is true or not, he or she will get the hint.
Leave me alone, please.	**Laissez-moi tranquille, s'il vous plaît.**
	les-say mwah trahN-keel seel voo pleh
	Polite and to to the point.
Get the heck out of here!	**Va voir ailleurs si j'y suis!**
	vah vwah ah-yur see zhee swee
	Literally: Go somewhere else— see if I'm there!
Go away!	**Casse-toi!**
	kahss twah
	It's brutal, but effective.

gay?

Looking for some alternative fun?

Are you gay?	**Es-tu gay?**
	eh-tew gay
Do you like men / women?	**Aimes-tu les hommes♂ / les femmes♀?**
	em-tew lay fahm / lay-zum
Let's go to a gay bar.	**Allons dans un bar gay.**
	Ah-lohN dahN zaN bah gay.

He's gay.	**Il est gay / homosexuel.**
	eel eh gay / oh-moh-sex-ew-el
She's a lesbian.	**Elle est lesbienne / homosexuelle.**
	el eh lez-bee-en / oh-moh-sex-ew-el
Get out of the closet!	**Sors du placard!**
	sawr dew plah-kahr

"Gay Pride" is the name of a gay-rights demonstration that occurs every June in Paris and other large French cities. Gay men and women parade through the city, some wearing colorful costumes. Straight friends and family also demonstrate their support of gay lifestyles. "Gay Pride" has steadily gained in popularity—ever since a gay mayor of Paris participated in the event.

Gay guys and girls will feel completely at ease anywhere in Paris, but will have the most fun in the Marais. This district is jam-packed with bars, clubs, hotels, spas, and stores that cater to a gay clientele. Just about every gay bar in this neighborhood will have magazines that include listings of gay events around town—grab one, 'cause it's free!

Montréal is another hot spot for gay tourists. While there, be sure to stroll along the streets of the Village, a neighborhood teeming with gay bistros, cafés, clubs, and shops. If you're here in August, check out "Divers/Cité", the annual gay pride parade.

91

dating

Found a French lover? Here's how to tell your love story.

I made out with him.

J'ai flirté avec lui.
zhay fluh-tay ah-vek lwee
The verb "flirter" is taken from the English, to flirt. Flirt, in turn, comes from the French, "flueretter," which literally means to tell flowers.

I'm going out with her.

Je suis sorti avec elle.
zhuh swee saw-tee ah-vek el

I french-kissed him.

Je lui ai roulé un patin.
zhuh lwee ay roo-lay aN pah-taN
Literally: I rolled a skate to him.

We got naked.

On s'est mis à poil.
ohN seh mee ah pwahl
Literally: We wore only our body hair.

sex

A variety of ways to state the obvious…

We …

Nous …
noo

slept together.

avons couché ensemble.
ah-vohN coo-shay ahN-sahN-bluh

made love.

avons fait l'amour.
ah-vohN feh lah-moor

@#&!ed.

avons baisé / avons niqué.
ah-vohN bay-zay / ah-vohN nee-ka

safe sex

Protection is a must, in any language.

I use …
J'utilise …
zhew-tee-leez

condoms.
des capotes / préservatifs.
day kah-pawt / pray-zair-vah-teef

the pill.
la pilule.
lah pee-lewl

a diaphragm.
un diaphragme.
aN dyah-frahm

Have you been tested for HIV?
Tu as fait un test HIV?
tew ah feh aN test ahsh-ee-veh

break up

The best ways to end your summer fling…

It's over between us.
C'est fini entre nous.
seh fee-nee ahN-truh noo
Be firm!

Let's just be friends.
Soyons amis.
swah-yohN zah-mee
Say this only if you mean it.

I'm breaking up with you.
Je romps avec toi.
zhuh rohNp ah-vek twah
End of story…

closure

Did he or she dump you? Here are the nastiest things you can call your ex.

You're a scumbag.

T'es une ordure.
teh ewn aw-dewr
"T'es" is the quick and easy wa
to say, "tu es", you are.

You're a ...

T'es un ...
teh aN

pathetic guy.

minable ♂.
mee-nah-bluh

loser.

pauvre type ♂.
poh-vruh teep

You're a ...

T'es une ...
teh ewn

slut.

pouffiasse ♀.
poof-fyahss

bitch.

salope ♀.
sah-lawp

where to shop

Grab your wallet and go!

Are we going shopping?	**On va faire des courses?** *ohN vah fair day koors*
Do you want to go window shopping?	**Tu veux faire du lèche-vitrine?** *tew vuh fair dew lehsh-vee-treen*
Where's the main mall?	**Où est le grand centre commercial** *oo eh luh grahN sahN-truh kum-air-see-al*
I'm looking for …	**Je cherche …** *zhuh shairsh*
a boutique.	**une boutique.** *ewn boo-teek*
a department store.	**un grand magasin.** *aN grahN mah-gah-zaN*
a flea market.	**un marché aux puces.** *aN mahr-shay oh pewss*
a market.	**un marché.** *aN mahr-shay*
an outlet store.	**un magasin de marques dégriffée** *aN mah-gah-zaN duh mahrk day-gree-f…*
a second-hand store.	**une boutique d'articles d'occasio** *ewn boo-teek dahr-tee-cluh* *doh-kah-zee-ohN*
a vintage shop.	**une boutique de fringues vintag** *ewn boo-teek duh fraN-guh veen-tah…*
When does the … open / close?	**À quelle heure … ouvre-t-il / ferme-t-il?** *ah kel uhr … oo-vruh- teel / fairm-teel*

Where's …?	**Où est …?**
	oo eh
the bookstore	**la librairie**
	lah lee-brair-ee
the camera shop	**le magasin de photos**
	luh mah-gah-zaN duh foh-toh
the health food store	**le magasin de diététique**
	luh mah-gah-zaN duh dee-yay-tay-teek
the jewelry store	**la bijouterie**
	lah bee-zhoo-tree
the liquor store	**le marchands de vins**
	luh mah-shahN duh vaN
the market	**le marché**
	luh mahr-shay
the music store	**le magasin de disques**
	luh mah-gah-zaN duh deesk
the newsstand	**le kiosque à journaux**
	luh kee-osk a zhoor-noh
the pharmacy	**la pharmacie**
	lah fahr-mah-see
the shoe store	**le magasin de chaussures**
	luh mah-gah-zaN duh shoh-sewr
the souvenir store	**le magasin de souvenirs**
	luh mah-gah-zaN duh soo-vuh-neer
the sports store	**le magasin d'articles de sport**
	luh mah-gah-zaN dahr-tee-kluh duh spawr
Are you open in the evening?	**Êtes-vous ouvert le soir?**
	et voo zoo-vair luh swah

97

customer service

Ask the right questions.

| Where's …? | **Où est …?** |
| | *oo eh* |

| the escalator | **l'escalier roulant** |
| | *less-kahl-yay roo-lahN* |

| the store map | **le plan du magasin** |
| | *luh plahN dew mah-gah-zaN* |

| Where's …? | **Où se trouve …?** |
| | *oo suh-troov* |

| customer service | **le service clientèle** |
| | *luh sair-veess klee-ahN-tel* |

| the fitting room | **la cabine d'essayage** |
| | *lah kah-been dess-ay-ahzh* |

| the lingerie department | **le rayon lingerie** |
| | *luh ray-ohN laNzh-ree* |

| the men's department | **le rayon homme** |
| | *luh ray-ohN um* |

| the perfume / cosmetics department | **le rayon parfumerie** |
| | *luh ray-ohN pah-fewm-ree* |

the register	**la caisse**
	lah kess
the shoe department	**le rayon chaussures**
	luh ray-ohN shoh-sewr
the women's department	**le rayon femme**
	luh ray-ohN fahm

Where can I find …? **Où trouver …?**
oo troo-vay

boot-cut pants **un pantalon boot-cut**
aN pahN-tah-lohN boot-cut

jeans **des jeans**
day dzheen

a leather jacket **une veste en cuir**
ewn vest ahN kweer

low-rise pants **un pantalon taille basse**
aN pahN-tah-lohN tah-yuh bahss

a miniskirt **une mini-jupe**
ewn mee-nee zhewp

a polo shirt **un polo**
aN poh-loh

I'm looking for … **Je cherche …**
zhuh shairsh

a backpack. **un sac à dos.**
aN sahk ah doh

books / magazines. **des livres / magazines.**
day lee-vruh / mah-gah-zeen

CDs / DVDs. **des CD / DVD.**
day say-day / day-vay-day

sales help

Here's how to ask that cute salesperson for assistance.

| Can you help me? | **Pouvez-vous m'aider?** |
| | *poo-vay voo may-day* |

| Can I try this on? | **Est-ce que je peux essayer ça?** |
| | *ess kuh zhuh puh ess-ay-yay sah* |

| Where's the fitting room? | **Où sont les cabines d'essayage?** |
| | *oo sohN lay kah-been des-say-ahzh* |

| Could you show me …? | **Pouvez-vous me montrer …?** |
| | *poo-vay voo muh mohN-tray* |

| I'd like to buy … | **Je voudrais acheter …** |
| | *zhuh voo-dray ahsh-tay* |

---

yo! Looking for something in a particular color? Ask for it in…

beige	**beige** *behzh*	orange	**orange** *oh-rahNzh*
black	**noir** *nwahr*	pink	**rose** *rawz*
blue	**bleu** *bluh*	purple	**violet** *vee-oh-leh*
brown	**marron** *mah-rohN*	red	**rouge** *roozh*
gray	**gris** *gree*	white	**blanc** *blahN*
green	**vert** *vair*	yellow	**jaune** *zhohn*

FACT Shopping in France may be fun, but who said it was easy? If you're not happy with your purchase, few stores will give you your money back—at best, you'll get a store credit. And your better decide quickly—you only have a few days to make the exchange.

yo! You may want to fill in the blanks above with any of these items.

baseball cap	**une casquette de baseball**	*ewn kahs-ket duh baze-bawl*
bikini	**un bikini**	*aN bee-kee-nee*
bra	**un soutien-gorge**	*aN soo-tyaN gawzh*
briefs	**un slip**	*aN sleep*
boxers	**un boxer**	*aN box-air*
coat	**un manteau**	*aN mahN-toh*
denim jacket	**une veste en jean**	*ewn vess-tuh ahN dzheen*
dress	**une robe**	*ewn rawb*
halter top, tank top	**un débardeur**	*aN day-bahr-duhr*
jeans	**un jean**	*aN dzheen*

messenger bag	**une besace**
	ewn buh-zahss
shirt	**une chemise**
	ewn shuh-meez
shoes	**des chouzes**
	day shoes
	It's the slangy way to say it.
shorts	**un short**
	aN shawt
skirt	**une jupe**
	ewn zhewp
socks	**des chaussettes**
	day shoh-set
sunglasses	**des lunettes de soleil**
	day lew-net duh soh-lay
swim trunks	**un slip de bain**
	aN sleep duh baN
thong	**un string**
	an streeng
tight T-shirt	**un t-shirt moulant**
	an tee-shirt moo-lahN

FACT In France, the price you see on the tag is the price you pay: taxes are already included. "Les soldes", sales, happen only twice a year, after New Year's and in July. It is illegal to have "des soldes" in between these periods. However, you might find "des promotions", discounts on specific items in any store, at various times of the year.

at the register

Looking to part with your hard-earned dough? Here's the lingo
you need to make your purchase.

How much?

Combien ça coûte?
kohN-byaN sah koot

Where do I pay?

Où dois-je payer?
oo dwah-zhuh pay-yay

Do you accept travelers checks?

Acceptez-vous les chèques de voyage?
ahk-sep-tay voo lay shek duh vwah-yahzh

Sorry, I don't have enough money.

Je regrette, je n'ai pas assez d'argent.
zhuh ruh-gret zhuh nay pah zahs-say dah-zhahN

Could I have a receipt please?

Est-ce que je peux avoir un ticket de caisse?
ess kuh zhuh puh ah-vwah aN tee-keh duh kess

I think you've given me the wrong change.

Je crois que vous vous êtes trompé♂ / trompée♀ en me rendant la monnaie.
zhuh kwa kuh voo voo zet trohN-pay ahN muh rahN-dahN lah moh-nay

bargains

Put your negotiating skills to use.

Is this on sale?

C'est en solde?
set ahN sawld

That's too expensive.	**C'est trop cher.**
	seh troh shair
It's pricey.	**Ça raque.**
	sah rahk
	Literally: It pays.
Will you lower the price?	**Vous me faites un prix?**
	voo muh fet aN pree
Can you give me a discount?	**Vous me faites une remise?**
	voo muh fet ewn ruh-meez
Do you have anything cheaper?	**Avez-vous quelque chose de moins cher?**
	ah-vay voo kel-kuh shohz duh mwaN shair
I'll think about it.	**Je vais réfléchir.**
	zhuh vay ray-flay-sheer

 Use your bargaining power at "les marchés aux puces", flea markets, and "les marchés", markets, which are usually outdoors and move from neighborhood to neighborhood. Check out...

Marché de St-Ouen—it's one of the largest in Europe and boasts more than 2,500 vendors

Marché de Vanves—smaller than St-Ouen, but a great place it you're looking for tchotchkes

Marché d'Aligre—the oldest Paris flea market; get your fresh produce here

problems

Is there something wrong with your purchase?

This doesn't work.	**Ça ne marche pas.** *sah nuh mahsh pah*
Can you exchange this, please?	**Pouvez-vous échanger ceci, s'il vous plaît?** *poo-vay voo ay-shahN-zhay suh-see seel voo pleh*
I'd like a refund.	**Je voudrais être remboursé ♂ / remboursée ♀.** *zhuh voo-dray zet-ruh rahN-boor-say*
Here's the receipt.	**Voici le ticket de caisse.** *vwah-see luh tee-keh duh kess*
I don't have the receipt.	**Je n'ai pas le ticket de caisse.** *zhuh nay pah luh tee-keh duh kess*

at the drugstore

Not feeling well? Here's some help.

Where's the nearest (all-night) pharmacy?	**Où est la pharmacie (de garde) la plus proche?** *oo eh lah fahr-mah-see (duh gahd) lah plew prawsh*
Can you fill this prescription for me?	**Pouvez-vous me préparer cette ordonnance?** *poo-vay voo muh pray-pah-ray set aw-dun-ahNss*
How much should I take?	**Combien dois-je en prendre?** *kohN-byaN dwah-zhuh ahN prahN-druh*

| How often should I take it? | **Combien de fois dois-je le prendre**
kohN-byaN duh fwah dwah-zhuh luh prahN-druh |
| Are there any side effects? | **Y a-t-il des effets secondaires?**
ee-ah-teel day zay-feh suh-gohN-dair |
| What would you recommend for …? | **Qu'est-ce que vous me recommandez pour …?**
kess kuh voo muh ruh-kum-mahN-day poor |
| a cold | **le rhume**
luh rewm |
| a cough | **la toux**
lah too |
| diarrhea | **la diarrhée**
lah dee-ah-ray |
| a hangover | **la gueule de bois**
lah guhl duh bwah |
| hay fever | **le rhume des foins**
luh rewm day fwaN |
| insect bites | **les piqûres d'insectes**
lay pee-kewr daN-sekt |
| a sore throat | **le mal de gorge**
luh mahl duh gawzh |
| sunburn | **les coups de soleil**
lay koo duh soh-lay |
| motion sickness | **le mal des transports**
luh mahl day trahN-spawr |
| an upset stomach | **le mal de ventre**
luh mahl duh vahN-truh |

Can I get it without a prescription?	**Puis-je l'obtenir sans ordonnance?**
	pwee-zhuh lob-tuh-neer sahN zaw-dun-ahNss
Can I have …?	**Pouvez-vous me donner …?**
	poo-vay voo muh dun-nay
antiseptic cream	**une crème antiseptique**
	ewn krem ahN-tee-sep-teek
aspirin	**de l'aspirine**
	duh lahss-pee-reen
bandages	**un bandage**
	aN bahN-dahzh
condoms	**des préservatifs**
	day pray-zair-vah-teef
bug repellent	**une crème / lotion contre les insectes**
	ewn krem / loh-see-ohN kohN-truh lay zaN-sekt
painkillers	**des analgésiques**
	day zahn-ahl-zhay-zeek
vitamins	**des vitamines**
	day vee-tah-meen

toiletries

Forgot to pack something?

I'd like …	**Je voudrais …**
	zhuh voo-dray
aftershave.	**de la lotion après-rasage.**
	duh lah loh-see-ohN ah-preh rah-zazh

| I'd like … | | **Je voudrais …** |
| | | *zhuh voo-dray* |

conditioner.

de l'après-shampooing.
duh lah-preh-shahN-pwaN

deodorant.

un déodorant.
aN day-oh-daw-rahN

moisturizing cream.

de la crème hydratante.
duh lah krem ee-drah-tahNt

razor blades.

des lames de rasoir.
day lahm duh rah-zwah

sanitary napkins.

des serviettes hygiéniques.
day sair-vyet ee-zhyay-neek

shampoo.

du shampooing.
dew shahN-pwaN

soap.

du savon.
dew sah-vohN

sun block.

de l'écran total.
duh lay-krahN toh-tahl

suntan lotion.

de la crème solaire.
duh lah krem soh-lair

tampons.

des tampons.
day tahN-pohN

tissues.

des mouchoirs en papier.
day moo-shwah ahN pah-pyay

toilet paper.

du papier toilette.
dew pah-pyay twah-let

toothpaste.

du dentifrice.
dew dahN-tee-freess

 Did you just see a shop with a big green glowing cross in front of it? That would be the pharmacy. Many are closed in the evening and on weekends, so if you're desperate for one you'll find a list of "pharmacies de garde", emergency pharmacies, in the window of any pharmacy or in the local newspaper.

make-up

Ladies, get all dolled up.

I need some …	**J'ai besoin de/d' …** *zhay buh zwaN duh/d'*
blush.	**blush.** *bluhsh*
eyeliner.	**eye liner.** *eye line-air*
eye shadow.	**ombre à paupières.** *ohM-bruh ah poh-pyair*
foundation.	**fond de teint.** *fohN duh taN*
lipgloss / lipstick.	**gloss / rouge à lèvres.** *glawss / roozh ah lev-ruh*
mascara.	**mascara.** *mah-scah-rah*
powder.	**poudre.** *poo-druh*

camera shop

Admit it, you're a tourist. You'll need these.

I'm looking for a disposable camera.

Je cherche un appareil photo jetable.
zhuh shairsh aN nah-pah-ray foh-toh zhuh-tah-bluh

Do you sell ... for digital cameras?

Est-ce que vous vendez des ... pour appareils photo numériques?
ess kuh voo vahN-day day ... poor ahp-pah-ray foh-toh new-mair-eek

memory cards

cartes mémoire
kahrt may-mwah

batteries

piles
peel

When will the photos be ready?

Quand est-ce que les photos seront prêtes?
kahN tess-kuh lay foh-toh suh-rohN pret

TECH TALK

internet café

Stay in touch with friends and family at home.

Is there an internet café near here?	**Y a-t-il un cybercafé par ici?** *ee ah-teel aN see-bair kah-fay pahr ee-see*
Can I access the internet here?	**Est-ce que je peux accéder à Internet d'ici?** *ess-kuh zhuh puh ahk-seh-day ah aN-tair-net dee-see*
What are the charges per hour?	**C'est combien par heure?** *seh kohN-byaN pah uhr*
How do I log on?	**Comment est-ce que je me connecte?** *kohN-mahN ess kuh zhuh muh koh-nekt*
I'd like to send a message by e-mail.	**Je voudrais envoyer un message par e-mail.** *zhuh voo-dray ahN-vwah-yay aN meh-sahzh pahr ee-mail*
What's your e-mail address?	**Quelle est ton adresse e-mail?** *kel eh tohN ah-dress ee-mail*
Check out …	**Tu as vu …** *tew ah vew*
this cool computer.	**ce super ordinateur / ordi.** *suh sew-pair aw-dee-nah-tuhr / aw-dee*
this cool laptop.	**ce super portable.** *suh sew-pair paw-tah-bluh*
this cool mouse.	**cette super souris.** *set sew-pair soo-ree*
Turn it on.	**Allume-le.** *ah-lewm luh*

Click here!	**Clique ici!**
	kleek ee-see
I'm going to …	**Je vais …**
	zhuh vay
go online.	**me connecter (à Internet).**
	muh koh-nek-tay (ah aN-tair-net)
send an e-mail.	**envoyer un e-mail.**
	ahN-vwah-yay aN nee-mail
You need to logout / reboot.	**Tu dois te déconnecter / redémarrer.**
	tew dwah tuh day-koh-nek-tay /
	ruh-day-mah-ray
My computer crashed.	**Mon ordi a planté.**
	mohN naw-dee ah plahN-tay

yo! Where is that internet café? For up-to-the-minute info on locations, try a www seach. If you're already at your French-speaking destination, find the local Tourist Information Office; it'll provide you with names, addresses, and directions for cybercafés. Worst comes to worst, walk around and read the signs. You're bound to find a few in every city and town.

laptop

Brought your own laptop? You might need these questions.

| Does this hotel / café have Wi-Fi®? | **Y a-t-il une connexion Wi-Fi® dans cet hôtel / ce café?** |
| | *ee ah-teel ewn koh-nek-see-ohN wee-fee dahN set oh-tel / suh kah-fay* |

Where is the closest hotspot?	**Où est le point d'accès Wi-Fi® le plus proche?**
	oo eh luh pwahN dahk-seh wee-fee luh plew prawsh
Is there a connection fee?	**La connexion est-elle payante?**
	lah koh-nek-see-ohN eh-tel pay-ahNt
Do I have to register?	**Est-ce que je dois m'inscrire?**
	ess kuh zhuh dwah maN-skreer

yo! Sitting next to a cutie at a French-speaking internet café or Wi-Fi® area? Spark his or her interest with these.

What's your favorite …?	**Quel est … préféré♂ / préférée♀?**
	kel eh … pray-fair-ay
chatroom	**ton chatroom**
	tohN chaht-room
webpage	**ta page web**
	tah pahzh web
website	**ton site**
	tohN seet
Can you …?	**Tu peux …?**
	tew puh
IM someone	**IM / dialoguer en direct**
	ee-em / dee-ah-law-gay ahN dee-rekt
send me an e-mail	**m'envoyer un e-mail**
	mahN-vwah-yay aN nee-mail
scroll up / down	**dérouler le texte**
	day-roo-lay luh text

yo! When visiting a chat room, keep in mind these abbreviations and expressions.

slt [Salut.]
Hi.

biz [Bisous.]
X [Kiss.]

dsl [Désolé.]
Sorry.

ASV [age, sexe, ville]
A/S/L [age, sex, location]
Start your chat by asking about 'em.

kékina [Qu'est-ce qu'il y a?]
RUOK [Are you OK?]
What's the matter?

dak [D'accord.]
OK

MDR [mort de rire]
LOL [laugh out loud]
Literally: dead from laughing

c ça [C'est ça!]
Really!
Literally: That's it!

l'S tomB [Laisse tomber.]
NP [No problem.]
Literally: Drop it.

A12C4 [À un de ces quatre.]
CU [See you.]
Literally: See you one of these [four] days.

@+ [À plus tard.]
CUL8R [See you later.]

instant messaging

Do you require instant gratification?

Bloquer	Ajouter un contact	Parler	Info	Envoyer
Block	Add buddy	Talk	Get info	Send

phone call

From public to private, the language you need to make your call.

I'd like a phonecard.

Je voudrais une télécarte / carte de téléphone.
zhuh voo-dray ewn tay-lay-kahrt / kahrt duh tay-lay-fun

I need to make a phone call.	**Je dois téléphoner à quelqu'un.** *zhuh dwah tay-lay-fun-ay ah kel-kaN*
Can I …?	**Je peux …?** *zhuh puh*
get your number	**prendre ton numéro** *prahN-druh tohN new-mair-oh* *A casual way to ask for digits.*
call you	**t'appeler** *tah-play*
make a call	**passer un coup de fil** *pah-say an coo duh feel*
I'll give you a call.	**Je t'appellerai.** *zhuh tah-pell-uh-ray*
Here's my number.	**Voilà mon numéro.** *vwah-lah mohN new-mair-oh*
Call me.	**Appelle-moi.** *ah-pell-mwah*
Where's the nearest phone booth?	**Où est la cabine téléphonique la plus proche?** *oo eh lah kah-been tay-lay-fun-eek lah plew prawsh*
May I use your phone?	**Est-ce que je peux me servir de votre téléphone?** *ess kuh zhuh puh muh sair-veer duh voh-truh tay-lay-fun*
It's an emergency.	**C'est urgent.** *set ewr-zhahN*
What's the number for Information?	**Quel est le numéro des Renseignements?** *kel eh luh new-mair-oh day rahN-sen-yuh-mahN*

I'd like to call collect.	**Je voudrais faire un appel en P.C.V.** *zhuh voo-dray fair aN nah-pell ahN pay* *say vay* *You can't make a collect call within France; you can call collect to countries outside France that accept 'em.*
Hello?	**Allô?** *ah-loh* *Say this when you answer the phone.*
Yes.	**Oui.** *wee* *If you don't want to say "Allô?" go for this one.*
It's …	**C'est …** *seh* *Just add your name.*
It's me!	**C'est moi!** *seh mwah*
Could I speak with …?	**Est-ce que je pourrais parler à …?** *ess kuh zhuh poor-ay pah-lay ah* *Formal, but to the point.*
I'd like to speak to …	**Je voudrais parler à …** *zhuh voo-dray pah-lay ah* *A little less uptight than the entry above.*
Can I leave a message?	**Je peux laisser un message?** *zhuh puh less-ay aN meh-sahzh* *Hope he or she calls you back.*
Hold on, please.	**Ne raccrochez pas, s'il vous plaît.** *nuh rah-krawsh-ay pah seel voo pleh*

When will he / she be back?	**Quand reviendra-t-il♂ / elle♀ ?**
	kahN ruh-vyaN-drah teel / tel
	You're desperate to talk to him or her, huh?
Will you tell him / her that I called?	**Pouvez-vous lui dire que j'ai appelé?**
	poo-vay voo lwee deer kuh zhay ah-play
	Is he or she avoiding you?
My name is …	**Je m'appelle …**
	zhuh mah-pell

bye!

End that phone conversation with class.

I'll be in touch.	**Je te téléphonerai.**
	zhuh tuh tay-lay-fun-ray
Good-bye.	**Au revoir.**
	oh ruh-vwah
Gotta go.	**J'y vais.**
	zhee veh
	You're in a rush to get off the phone!
Later.	**À plus.**
	ah plews
	A short and sweet ending.
Love you.	**Je t'embrasse.**
	zhuh tahN-brahss
	Literally: I kiss you.
	Use this one with friends and family.
Let's talk later.	**On s'appelle.**
	ohN sah-pel
	This can mean: I won't call you.

Send someone you love "les textos", text messages.

slt cv? [Salut, ça va?]
Hi, how are you?

m jvb [Moi, je vais bien.]
I'm fine.

keske C [Qu'est-ce que c'est?]
What is it?

koi29? [Quoi de neuf?]
What's up?

je t'M [Je t'aime.]
I love you.

rstp [Réponds s'il te plaît.]
Answer please.

Cpa5p [C'est pas sympa.]
That's not nice.

j'tapL + tard [Je t'appelle plus tard.]
I'll call you later.

@2m1 [À demain.]
See you tomorrow.

FACT Haven't used a public phone in a while, huh?! Here's how to make a call from the corner phone.

FRENCH-SPEAKING EUROPE

You'll find two kinds of telephone booths where you can make your local and international calls: coin-operated (these are few and far between) and card-operated. Since you're more than likely to be using the card-operated phone, here's how to work it: buy a "télécarte" or "carte de téléphone" from a newsstand, tobacco shop, or post office. Insert the card and follow the instructions on the screen.

Décrocher	Lift the receiver
Insérer votre carte	Insert your card
Composer le numéro	Dial the number
Raccrocher	Hang up

You can reach the international operator by dialing 00 32 12.

In France, Belgium, and Switzerland, make an international call by dialing 00 + country code + number. Country codes are: Australia = 61, UK = 44, US and Canada = 1.

QUEBEC PROVINCE, CANADA

Public phones take coins. You can also make a call using a pre-paid phone card or calling card; if you didn't bring your own, buy a "La Puce" phone pass from any "Espace Bell" phone service shop. Need an operator? Dial 0.

To call anywhere in North America, just dial 1 + area code + number. To call abroad, dial 011 + country code + number.

snail mail

Mail your stuff from "La Poste".

Where is the post office? **Où est le bureau de poste?**
oo eh luh bew-roh duh pawst
Ask a cutie—he or she might
even take you there personally.

What time does the
post office open / close? **À quelle heure ouvre / ferme
la poste?**
ah kel uhr oov-ruh / fairm lah pawst

A stamp for this postcard,
please. **Un timbre pour cette carte
postale, s'il vous plaît.**
aN taN-bruh poor set kahrt paws-tahl
seel voo pleh

What's the postage for
a letter to …? **Quel est le tarif d'une lettre pour …?**
kel eh luh tah-reef dewn let-truh poor

I want to send this
package … **Je voudrais envoyer ce paquet …**
zhuh voo-dray ahN-vwah-yay suh pah-keh

by airmail. **par avion.**
pahr ah-vyohN

by express mail. **en exprès.**
aN nex-press

the scoop

*Tired of the same ol' boring postcards? Well, in France, you
can make your own! France's post office offers an online
service in which you can personalize a postcard using your
own photo or an image from the post office's collection. Just
go to **www.laposte.fr** for more information.*

DICTIONARY
French ► English

A

à l'heure on time

à quelle heure what time *also* when

abîmé *m* / **abîmée** *f* damaged

accès *m* **internet** Internet access

accès *m* access *also* entrance

accident *m* accident

acheter to buy

acide sour

addition *f* check (in a restaurant)

adresse *f* address

adresse *f* **e-mail** e-mail address

ADSL DSL

aéroport *m* airport

agression *f* mugging

aider to help

aïgo bouïdo Provençal garlic soup

ail *m* garlic

aimer to love

aller to go

allergie *f* allergy

aller-retour *m* round-trip (ticket)

aller-simple *m* one-way (ticket)

allumer to turn on (a machine)

allumettes *f* matches

alpinisme *m* mountain-climbing

amer *m* / **amère** *f* bitter

américain *m* / **américaine** *f* American

ami *m* / **amie** *f* friend

amour *m* love

analgésiques *f* painkillers

anglais English

Angleterre *f* England

annuler to cancel

anorexique anorexic

antiseptique antiseptic

apéro *m (slang)* before-dinner drink

appareil photo *m* camera

appareil photo *m* **jetable** disposable camera

appareil photo *m* **numérique** digital camera

appel *m* phone call

appeler to call

après-shampooing *m* conditioner

arbitre *m* referee

argent *m* money

arrêt *m* stop

arrêté *m* / **arrêtée** *f* arrested

arrêter to stop

arrhes *f* deposit (advance fee)

arrivées *f* arrivals

arriver to arrive

artichaut *m* artichoke

aspirine *f* aspirin

assaisonnement *m* seasoning

assiette *f* plate

assurance *f* insurance

attaque *f* attack

attendre to wait

auberge *m* **de jeunesse** youth hostel

123

auberge *m* inn
aujourd'hui today
Australie *f* Australia
autobus *m* bus
automatique automatic
avion *m* airplane
avocat *m* lawyer
avoir besoin (de) to need

B

bâfrer *(slang)* to eat a lot
bagage *m* luggage
bain *m* bath *also* bathtub
baiser *m* kiss
bandage *m* bandage
banque *f* bank
bar *m* bar
basket *m* basketball
beau *m* / **belle** *f* beautiful
beaux arts *m* fine arts
beige beige
belvédère *m* viewpoint
beurre *m* butter
bicyclette *f* bicycle
bien well
bière *f* beer
bijouterie *f* jewelry store
bijoux *m* jewelry
bikini *m* bikini
billet *m* ticket
biscuit *m* cookie
bistro *m* diner (eatery)
blanc *m* / **blanche** *f* white
blanquette de veau veal stew

bleu blue
bœuf *m* beef
boire to drink
boisson *f* **gazeuse** soda
boisson *f* drink
boîte *f* **(de nuit)** (night) club
bon *m* / **bonne** *f* good
boui-boui *m* *(slang)* dive (eatery)
bouillabaisse seafood soup,
 specialty of Marseilles
boulimique bulimic
bouteille *f* bottle
boxe *f* boxing
boxer *m* boxers
brasserie *f* café, pub
brassière *f* bra
bruyant *m* / **bruyante** *f* noisy
buffet *m* snack bar, buffet
bureau *m* office *also* desk
bureau *m* **de change** currency
 exchange office
bureau *m* **de location de voitures**
 car rental office
bureau *m* **de poste** post office
bureau *m* **des objets trouvés**
 lost-and-found
bureau *m* **des renseignements**
 information desk
bus *m* bus

C

cabine *f* **d'essayage** fitting room
cabine *f* **téléphonique** phone
 booth

câble *m* broadband cable
cacahuète *f* peanut
cadeau *m* gift
café *m* café *also* coffee
caisse *f* cash register
calorie *f* calorie
cambriolage *m* theft
camping *m* campsite
Canada *m* Canada
canard *m* duck
canot *m* **automobile** motorboat
capote *f* condom
carafe *f* carafe
carnet *m* **(de tickets)** booklet of Métro or bus tickets
carotte *f* carrot
carte *f* map *also* card
carte d'étudiant internationale International Student Card
carte de crédit credit card
carte des vins wine list
carte mémoire memory card
carte postale postcard
casino *m* casino
casquette *f* cap
ce soir tonight
cendrier *m* ashtray
centre *m* **commercial** mall
centre-ville *m* the center of town
chaîne *f* stereo
chaise *f* chair
chambre *f* bedroom *also* hotel room
chambre *f* **à un lit** single room

chambre *f* **pour deux personnes** double room
champignon *m* mushroom
change *m* exchange
changer to change, exchange
charbon *m* charcoal
charcuterie *f* café serving ready-made food to go
chariots *m* **à bagages** luggage carts
château *m* castle
chaud *m* **/ chaude** *f* hot
chauffage *m* heating system
chaussettes *f* socks
chaussure *f* shoe
chemise *f* shirt
chèque *m* check
chèque de voyage travelers check
cher *m* **/ chère** *f* expensive
chercher to look for
chirurgie *f* **esthétique** plastic surgery
chocolat *m* chocolate
cholestérol *m* cholesterol
chou *m* cabbage
cigarette *f* cigarette
cimetière *m* cemetery
ciné(ma) *m* movie theater
cinq five
citron *m* lemon
classe *f* class
clé *f* key
climatisation *f* air conditioning

clope *m (slang)* cigarette

club *m* **gay** gay club

coffre-fort *m* safe

combien how much *also* how many

combien de temps how long (time)

comédie *f* comedy

commander to order

commencer to begin, start

comment how

commissariat *m* police station

composter votre billet validate your ticket

comprendre to understand

compris *m* / **comprise** *f* included

compte *m* account

compteur *m* meter (of taxi)

concert *m* concert

concombre *m* cucumber

conduire to drive

confirmer to confirm

confiture *f* jelly, jam

(se) connecter to log on (computer)

connexion *f* dial-up Internet connection

consigne *f* baggage check

consulat *m* consulate

contravention *f* speeding ticket

contrôle *m* **de sécurité** security check

contrôle *m* **des passeports** passport control

coq au vin chicken in wine sauce

cornichon *m* pickle

couleur *f* color

couloir *m* corridor, hallway, aisle

coup *m* **de téléphone** phone call

coups *m* **de soleil** sunburn

court *m* / **courte** *f* short (thing)

couteau *m* knife

coûter to cost

couverture *f* blanket

crabe *m* crab

crème *f* **anglaise** custard

crème *f* **antiseptique** antiseptic cream

crème *f* **contre les insectes** bug repellent

crème *f* **hydratante** moisturizing cream

crème *f* **solaire** suntan lotion

crêpe *f* thin pancake

crêperie *f* crêpe stand

crevette *f* shrimp

croque monsieur toasted ham and cheese sandwich

cuillère *f* spoon

cuire to cook

cuisses de grenouille frog legs

culotte *f* panties

cybercafé *m* Internet café

cyclomoteur *m* moped

D

dans in
danser to dance
décaféiné decaffeinated
déclarer to declare
dedans inside
dégoûtant *m* **/ dégoûtante** *f*
  disgusting
dehors outside
déjeuner *m* lunch
délicieux *m* **/ délicieuse** *f*
  delicious
demain tomorrow
demander to ask, request
démarrer to start (a car)
dentifrice *m* toothpaste
déodorant *m* deodorant
dépanneuse *f* tow truck
départs *m* departures
dépôt *m* deposit (in bank)
dernier *m* **/ dernière** *f* last
descendre to go downstairs *also*
  to get off
deux two
devise *f* currency
diabétique diabetic
diaphragme *m* diaphragm
diarrhée *f* diarrhea
dîner *m* dinner *also* to dine
dire to say, to tell
directeur *m* **/ directrice** *f*
  manager
discothèque *f* dance club

distance *f* distance
distributeur *m* **automatique** ATM
  (cash machine)
dix ten
douane *f* customs
doublé dubbed
douche *f* shower
doux *m* **/ douce** *f* sweet
douze twelve
drame *m* drama
draps *m* bedding
droite right
durer to last

E

eau *f* water
eau *f* **minérale** mineral water
Écosse *f* Scotland
écouteurs *m* earphones,
  headphones
écran *m* **total** sun block
écrire to write
édulcorant *m* (artificial)
  sweetener
effacer to clear, erase
église *f* church
embrasser to kiss
emmener to take (someone)
en exprès express mail
en liquide in cash
en pression draft (beer)
en solde *m* on sale
encaisser to cash
enfant *m* child

enfermer to lock

ennuyeux *m* / **ennuyeuse** *f* boring

enregistrement *m* check-in

entrée *f* entrance *also* appetizer

envoyer to send

épeler to spell

épicerie *f* grocery store

épilation *f* wax (hair removal)

époustouflant *m* / **époustouflante** *f* breathtaking

équipe *m* team

erreur *f* mistake

escargot *m* snail

espace *m* **Wi-Fi®** Wi-Fi® area

espresso *m* espresso

essence *f* gas(oline)

(chez l')esthéticienne *f* beauty salon

États-Unis *m* U.S.

éteindre to turn off (a machine)

étranger *m* / **étrangère** *f* foreign

étudiant *m* / **étudiante** *f* student

excursion *f* excursion, tour

exprès on purpose

extra super

F

faire to do *also* to make

faire la fête to party

faire la queue to wait in line

famille *f* family

fantastique brilliant

fatigué *m* / **fatiguée** *f* tired

femme *f* woman *also* wife

fenêtre *f* window

fermer to close *also* to lock

fête *f* party

feu *m* fire

figure *f* face

film *m* movie

foie *m* liver

fond *m* **de teint** foundation (make-up)

football *m* soccer

fourchette *f* fork

fraise *f* strawberry

frère *m* brother

frites *f* fries

froid *m* / **froide** *f* cold

fromage *m* cheese

fruit *m* fruit

fumer to smoke

fumeur smoker *also* smoking (section)

G

galerie *f* **d'art** art gallery

garder to keep

gare *f* station

garo *f* *(slang)* cigarette

gâteau *m* cake

gauche left

gay gay

gaz *m* **butane** butane gas

gazeuse carbonated

gin tonic *m* gin and tonic

glacé *m* / **glacée** *f* iced

glace *f* ice *also* ice cream

glaçon *m* ice cube

gloss *m* à lèvres lip gloss

gorge *f* throat

goûter *m* traditional afternoon snack

grand *m* / **grande** *f* large, big, tall

grand magasin *m* department store

Grande-Bretagne *f* Britain

gratuit *m* / **gratuite** *f* free (of cost)

grenouille *f* frog

gris *m* / **grise** *f* gray

gros *m* / **grosse** *f* fat

gueule *f* de bois *(slang)* hangover (literally: a wooden head)

guichet *m* ticket office

H

haltères *m* weights

haricot bean

haute cuisine *f* fine, traditional French food

hépatite *f* hepatitis

herpès *m* herpes

heure *f* hour

hippodrome *m* racetrack

homard *m* lobster

homme man

homosexuel *m* / **homosexuelle** *f* gay

horaires *m* schedule

hors taxes duty-free

hôtel *m* hotel

hôtel *m* de ville town hall

hôtel garni bed and breakfast

huit eight

huître *f* oyster

hydratant *m* / **hydratante** *f* moisturizing

I

ici here

incroyable amazing

insecte *m* insect

insérer to insert

intéressant *m* / **intéressante** *f* interesting

Internet *m* Internet

Irlande *f* Ireland

J

jambe *f* leg

jambon *m* ham

jardin *m* garden

jaune yellow

jeans *m* jeans

jeu *m* game

(faire du) jogging to jog

jour *m* day

journée *f* day

jupe *f* skirt

jus *m* juice

129

K

kayak *m* kayaking
kilométrage *m* mileage
kiosque *m* **à journaux** newsstand

L

laid *m* / **laide** *f* ugly
lait *m* milk
laitue *f* lettuce
lame *f* **de rasoir** razor blade
lampe *f* **de poche** / **électrique** flashlight
lapin *m* rabbit
lard *m* bacon
lavabo *m* sink
lecteur *m* **de CD** CD player
lecteur *m* **MP3** MP3 player
lentement slowly
lesbienne *f* lesbian
lettre *f* letter
lèvres *m* lips
libérer la chamber to check out (of hotel)
librairie *f* bookstore
libre free (available)
ligne *f* line
limonade *f* lemonade
lit *m* bed
livre *m* book
loin far
long *m* / **longue** *f* long (distance, size)
lotion *f* lotion
louer to rent

lumière *f* light
lunettes *f* glasses

M

madame *f* ma'am
mademoiselle *f* miss (young or unmarried woman)
magasin *m* shop, store
magnifique magnificent
maigre skinny
maillot *m* sports jersey
main *f* hand
maintenant now
maître-nageur *m* lifeguard
mal badly
mal *m* **de gorge** sore throat
mal *m* **de l'air** airsickness
mal *m* **de ventre** upset stomach
mal *m* **des transports** motion sickness
malade ill, sick
maladie *f* **sexuellement transmise (MST)** sexually transmitted disease (STD)
manger to eat
manquer to miss
manteau *m* coat
manucure *f* manicure
maquereau *m* mackerel
maquillage *m* make-up
marchand *m* **de vins** liquor store
marchandise *f* merchandise
marché *m* market
marché *m* **aux puces** flea market

marcher to work (something)

mari husband

marron brown

massage *m* massage

match *m* **(de ...)** (sports) game

matelas *m* mattress

mauvais *m* / **mauvaise** *f* bad

mécanicien *m* mechanic

médecin *m* doctor

même same

menotté *m* / **menottée** *f*
handcuffed

menthe *f* mint

menu *m* menu

mère mother

Métro *m* subway

miel *m* honey

milk shake *m* milkshake

mobylette *f* moped

moins cher *m* / **moins chère** *f*
less expensive

monnaie *f* change (money)

monsieur sir

montre *f* watch

monument *m* memorial

morue *f* cod

mouchoirs *m* **en papier** tissues

moules *f* mussels

mousse *f* **au chocolat** chocolate
mousse

moutarde *f* mustard

musée *m* museum

musique *f* music

N

nager to swim

(faire de la) natation *f* to swim

nettoyage *m* **de peau** facial

neuf nine

neuf *m* / **neuve** *f* new

nez *m* nose

noir *m* / **noire** *f* black

nombril *m* belly button

non no

non gazeuse non-carbonated

non-fumeur non-smoking

note *f* **détaillée** itemized bill

note *f* bill

nourriture *f* food

nouveau *m* / **nouvelle** *f* new

nouvelle cuisine *f* fine modern
French food

nuigrav *f (slang)* cigarette

numéro *m* **de confirmation**
confirmation number

O

obèse obese

objet *m* object, item

occupé *m* / **occupée** *f* taken

oeil *m* eye

œuf *m* egg

office *m* **du tourisme** tourist
information office

oignon *m* onion

ombre *f* **à paupières** eyeshadow

ongle *m* nail

onze eleven

opéra *m* opera *also* opera house

orange *f* orange

ordinateur *m* computer

ordonnance *f* prescription

ordure *f* scumbag

oreille *f* ear

oreiller *m* pillow

où where

oui yes

ouvert *m* / **ouverte** open

P

(faire un appel en) P.C.V. to call collect

page *f* **web** webpage

pain *m* bread

pain *m* **grillé** toast

palais *m* palace

pamplemousse *m* grapefruit

panneau *m* sign

pantalon *m* pants, trousers

papier *m* **toilette** toilet paper

paquet *m* package

par avion airmail

par heure per hour

par jour per day

par semaine per week

parapluie *m* umbrella

parasol *m* beach umbrella

parc *m* park

parents *m* parents

parfumerie *f* perfume shop

parler to speak

partir to depart, leave

passeport *m* passport

passe-temps *m* hobby

pâté liver purée

pâtisserie *f* pastry shop

patron *m* / **patronne** *f* manager

pauvre low (nutrition)

payer to pay

peau *f* skin

pédicure *f* pedicure

peigne *m* comb

pellicule *f* film (photography)

perdu *m* / **perdue** *f* lost

père *m* father

petit *m* / **petite** *f* small (person, thing) *also* short (a person)

petit ami *m* / **petite amie** *f* boyfriend / girlfriend

petit déjeuner *m* breakfast

petit pain *m* roll (bread)

petite monnaie *f* small change

petits pois *m* peas

pharmacie *f* pharmacy

photo *f* photo

pièce *f* **de théâtre** play

pied *m* foot

pile *f* battery

pilule *f* (birth-control) pill

pinard *m* cheap wine

piqûres *f* **d'insectes** insect bites, stings

piscine *f* swimming pool

place *f* seat *also* plaza, square

plage *f* beach

plan *m* map
planche *f* **de surf** surfboard
plat *m* meal *also* main course
plat *m* **/ platte** *f* flat
plein full
plonger to dive
pneu *m* tire
poire *f* pear
poisson *m* fish
poivre *m* pepper
police *f* police
pomme *f* **de terre** potato
pomme *f* apple
porc *m* pork
porte *f* door *also* gate
portefeuille *m* wallet
porte-monnaie *m* wallet
poudre *f* powder
poulet *m* chicken
pour emporter to go (a meal)
préféré *m* **/ préférée** *f* favorite
premier *m* **/ première** *f* first
première classe *f* first class
prendre to take (something)
près near, close
préservatif *m* condom
priorité *f* right-of-way
pris *m* **/ prise** *f* taken
prison *f* jail
prix *m* price
prochain *m* **/ prochaine** *f* next
proche near, close

profiteroles cream puffs
programme *m* program
propre clean

Q

quai *m* platform (in train station)
quatre four
quel *m* **/ quelle** *f* which *also* what
queue *f* line
quiche *f* egg and cheese tart

R

ragoût meat stew, generally served in gravy with vegetables
rameur *m* rowing machine
rasoir *m* razor
rater to miss
rayon *m* department
recommander to recommend
reçu *m* receipt
réduction *f* discount
réduit reduced
remboursement *m* refund
repas *m* meal
répéter to repeat
réservation *f* reservation
réserver to reserve
restaurant *m* restaurant
resto *m (slang)* restaurant
retard *m* delay
retrait *m* withdrawal (of money)
(se) réveiller to wake up
revenir to come back, to return

rhum *m* rum

rhume *m* **des foins** hay fever

rhume *m* cold (illness)

rien nothing

robe *f* dress

robinet *m* faucet

rognon *m* kidney

romantique romantic

rose pink *also* rose

rouge red

rouge *m* **à lèvres** lipstick

routier *m* roadside diner

rues *f* **commerçantes** shopping areas

ruines *f* ruins

S

s'il vous plaît please

sable *m* sand

sac *m* **à dos** backpack

sac *m* **à main** purse

sac *m* **de couchage** sleeping bag

sachet *m* bag

salade *f* salad

salle *f* room

sans without

sans gluten gluten-free

sauce *f* sauce

saucisse *f* sausage

saumon *m* salmon

saut *m* **à l'élastique** bungee jumping

saut *m* **en parachute** skydiving

savon *m* soap

science *f* science

scooter *m* **de mer** jet ski

se connecter to log on (computer)

sec *m* **/ sèche** *f* dry

sécurité *f* security

seins *m* breasts

sel *m* salt

self-service *m* self-service (gas station) *also* buffet

semaine *f* week

sept seven

serré *m* **/ serrée** *f* tight

serrure *f* lock

service de chambre room service

service de nettoyage laundry service

service *m* service

serviette *f* napkin

serviette *f* **de bain** bath towel

serviette *f* **hygiénique** sanitary napkin

sexe *m* sex

shampooing *m* shampoo

short *m* shorts

SIDA *m* AIDS

siège *m* seat

signaler to report (to police)

six six

ski *m* **nautique** waterski

slip *m* briefs

sodium *m* sodium

sœur *f* sister

soin *m* **des pieds** pedicure

soir *m* evening, night

solde *m* sale

sole *f* sole

soleil *m* sun

sombre dark

sommelier *m* wine waiter

sortie *f* exit

soufflé *m* **au chocolat** chocolate soufflé

sôulé *m* **/ sôulée** *f* drunk

soupe *f* soup

sourcil *m* eyebrow

sous-titre *m* subtitle

soutien-gorge *m* bra

souvenir *m* souvenir

spécialités *f* **régionales** traditional local dishes

station *f* station *also* stop

steak *m* steak

string *m* thong

stupéfiant *m* **/ stupéfiante** *f* stunning

sucre *m* sugar

superbe superb

supermarché *m* supermarket

(faire du) surf to surf

sympa(thique) nice (person) *also* good (place)

syphilis *f* syphilis

T

tampon *m* tampon

tapis *m* **de course** treadmill

tarif *m* postage, rate

tasse *f* cup

tatouer to tattoo

taux *m* **de change** exchange rate

taxe *f* tax, duty

taxi *m* taxi

tee-shirt *m* T-shirt

V

valise *f* suitcase

vanille *f* vanilla

veau *m* veal

végétalien *m* **/ végétalienne** *f* vegan

végétarien *m* **/ végétarienne** *f* vegetarian

vélo *m* bicycle

vélomoteur *m* moped

ventilateur *m* fan

ventre *m* stomach

verre *m* glass *also (slang)* shot (of liquor)

vert *m* **/ verte** *f* green

veste *f* jacket

vêtements *m* clothes

viande *f* meat

vieille ville *f* old town

vignoble *m* vineyard

ville *f* town

vin *m* wine

vinaigrette *f* salad dressing

viol *m* rape

violet *m* **/ violette** *f* purple

visite *f* **guidée** guided tour

visite *f* **touristique** sightseeing tour

vitamine *f* vitamin
vite fast, quickly
vodka *f* vodka
voiture *f* car
vol *m* flight
volé *m* / **volée** *f* stolen
voleur *m* thief
volley *m* volleyball
vomir to vomit
voyage *m* trip

W

week-end *m* weekend
whisky *m* whisky

Z

zone *f* **non-fumeur** non-smoking
area

DICTIONARY
English ➤ French

A

accident accident *m*

account compte *m*

address adresse *f*

aftershave lotion *f* après-rasage

AIDS SIDA *m*

air conditioning climatisation *f*

airmail par avion

airplane avion *m*

airport aéroport *m*

airsickness mal de l'air *m*

aisle seat siège *m* côté couloir

allergy allergie *f*

all-night pharmacy pharmacie *f* de garde

amazing incroyable

American américain *m* / américaine *f*

anorexic anorexique

antiseptic cream crème *f* antiseptique

aperitif apéritif *m*, *(slang)* apéro

appetizer entrée *f*

apple pomme *f*

arrested arrêté *m* / arrêtée *f*

arrivals arrivées *f*

to arrive arriver

art gallery galerie *f* d'art

artichoke artichaut *m*

artificial sweetener édulcorant *m*

ashtray cendrier *m*

aspirin aspirine *f*

ATM (cash machine) distributeur *m* automatique

attack attaque *f*

Australia Australie *f*

automatic automatique

available libre

avocado avocat *m*

B

backpack sac *m* à dos

bacon lard *m*

bad mauvais *m* / mauvaise *f*

bag sac, sachet *m*

baggage bagage *m*

bandage bandage *m*

bank banque *f*

bar bar *m*

to barf vomir

basketball basket *m*

bass (fish) bar *m*

bath bain *m*

bath towel serviette *f* de bain

bathroom les toilettes *f*

bathtub bain *m*

battery pile *f*

beach plage *f*

bean haricot *m*

beautiful beau *m* / belle *f*

beauty salon (chez l')esthéticienne

bed lit *m*

bed and breakfast hôtel *m* garni

137

bedding draps *m*

bedroom chambre *f*

beef bœuf *m*

beer bière *f*

begin commencer

beige beige

belly button nombril *m*

bicycle bicyclette *f*, vélo *m*

big grand *m* / grande *f*

bikini bikini *m*

bikini wax épilation *f* du maillot

bill note *f*, **(in a restaurant)** addition *f*

birth-control pill pilule *f*

bitter amer *m* / amère *f*

black noir *m* / noire *f*

blanket couverture *f*

blue bleu

book livre *m*

bookstore librairie *f*

boring ennuyeux *m* / ennuyeuse *f*

botanical garden jardin *m* botanique

bottle bouteille *f*

boxers boxer *m*

boxing boxe *f*

boyfriend petit ami *m*

bra brassière *f*, soutien-gorge *m*

bread pain *m*

to break casser

breakfast petit déjeuner *m*

breasts seins *m*

breathtaking époustouflant *m* / époustouflante *f*

briefs slip *m*

brilliant fantastique

Britain Grande-Bretagne *f*

brother frère *m*

brown marron

buffet buffet *m*, self (-service) *m*

bug insecte *m*

bulimic boulimique

bungee jumping saut *m* à l'élastique

bus autobus *m*, bus *m*

butane gas gaz *m* butane

butter beurre *m*

to buy acheter

C

cab taxi *m*

cabbage chou *m*

café café *m*

cake gâteau *m*

to call appeler

calorie calorie *f*

camera appareil photo *m*

camera shop magasin *m* de photos

campsite camping *m*

Canada Canada *m*

to cancel annuler

cap casquette *f*

car voiture *f*

carafe carafe *f*

card carte *f*

carrot carotte *f*

to cash (a check) encaisser (un chèque)

cash machine (ATM) distributeur *m* automatique

cash register caisse *f*

casino casino *m*

castle château *m*

CD player lecteur *m* de CD

cemetery cimetière *m*

center of town centre-ville *m*

chair chaise *f*

change monnaie *f*

charcoal charbon *m*

check chèque *m*

check (in a restaurant) addition *f*

check in l'enregistrement *m*

cheese fromage *m*

chicken poulet *m*

child enfant *m*

chocolate chocolat *m*

cholesterol cholestérol *m*

church église *f*

cigarette cigarette *f*, *(slang)* clope *m*, garo *f*, nuigrav *f*

clean propre

to clear effacer

to close fermer

close to près, proche

clothes vêtements *m*

clothing store magasin *m* de vêtements

(night) club boîte *f* (de nuit)

coat manteau *m*

cod morue *f*

coffee café *m*

cold froid *m* / froide *f*

collect call appel *m* en P.C.V.

color couleur *f*

comb peigne *m*

to come back revenir

comedy comédie *f*

computer ordinateur *m*

concert concert *m*

conditioner après-shampooing *m*

condom capote *f*, préservatif *m*

to confirm confirmer

confirmation number numéro *m* de confirmation

consulate consulat *m*

to cook cuire

cookie biscuit *m*

cosmetics department rayon *m* parfumerie

to cost coûter

cough toux *f*

cover charge payer pour rentrer

crab crabe *m*

credit card carte *f* de crédit

cucumber concombre *m*

cup tasse *f*

currency devise *f*

currency exchange office bureau *m* de change

custard crème *f* anglaise

customs douane *f*

cycling faire du vélo *m*

D

damaged abîmé *m* / abîmée *f*

dance club discothèque *f* / boîte *f* (de nuit)

to dance danser

dark sombre

day jour *m*

decaffeinated décaféiné

to declare déclarer

delay retard *m*

delicious délicieux *m* / délicieuse *f*

deodorant déodorant *m*

to depart partir

department (in store) rayon *m*

department store grand magasin *m*

departures départs *m*

deposit (in bank) dépôt *m*, **(advance fee)** arrhes *f*

desk bureau *m*

dessert dessert *m*

diabetic diabétique

dial-up internet connection connexion *f*

diaphragm diaphragme *m*

diarrhea diarrhée *f*

diet régime *m*

digital camera appareil photo *m* numérique

diner bistro *m*

dinner dîner *m*

discount réduction *f*

disgusting dégoûtant *m* / dégoûtante *f*

disposable camera appareil photo *m* jetable

distance distance *f*

dive (eatery) *(slang)* boui-boui *m*

doctor médecin *m*

door porte *f*

double room chambre *f* pour deux personnes

to download télécharger

downtown centre-ville *m*

draft (beer) en pression

drama drame *m*

dress robe *f*

dressing (salad) vinaigrette *f*

drink boisson *f*

to drink boire

to drive conduire

drugstore pharmacie *f*

drunk sôûlé *m* / sôûlée *f*

dry sec *m* / sèche *f*

dry (wine) brut

DSL internet access ADSL

dubbed doublé *m* / doublée *f*

duck canard *m*

duty (tax) taxe *f*

E

ear oreille *f*

earphones écouteurs *m*

to eat manger

economy class (on airplane) classe *f* économique

egg oeuf *m*

eight huit

eleven onze

e-mail address adresse f e-mail m

emergency urgence f

England Angleterre f

English anglais

entrance entrée f

to erase effacer

evening soir m

to exchange changer

excursion excursion f

exercise bike vélo m de salle

exit sortie f

expensive cher m / chère f

express mail en exprès

extra supplémentaire

eye oeil m

eye shadow ombre f à paupières

eyebrow sourcil m

F

face figure f

facial nettoyage m de peau

family famille f

fan ventilateur m

far loin

fare ticket m

fast vite

fat graisse f (n), gros m / grosse f (adj)

father père m

faucet robinet m

favorite préféré m / préférée f

to fill remplir

film (photography) pellicule f

fingernails ongles m des mains

first premier m / première f

first class première classe f

fish poisson m

fitness bike vélo m de salle

fitting room cabine f d'essayage

five cinq

flashlight lampe f de poche, lampe électrique

flat plat m / platte f

flea market marché m aux puces

flight vol m

food nourriture f

foot pied m

football football m américain

foreign étranger m / étrangère f

fork fourchette f

found trouvé m / trouvée f

foundation (make-up) fond m de teint

four quatre

free (available) libre, **(price)** gratuit m / gratuite f

fried egg oeuf m au plat

friend ami m / amie f

fries frites f

frog legs cuisses de grenouille

fruit fruit m

G

gallery galerie f

(sports) game match m (de ...) also jeu m

garden jardin m

garlic ail *m*

gas l'essence *f*

gate porte *f*

gay gay, homosexuel *m* / homosexuelle *f*

to get off (a bus, train, etc.) descendre

gift cadeau *m*

gin and tonic gin tonic *m*

girlfriend petite amie *f*

glass verre *m*

glasses lunettes *f*

gluten-free sans gluten

good bon *m* / bonne *f*

goods marchandises *f*

grapefruit pamplemousse *m*

gray gris *m* / grise *f*

green vert *m* / verte *f*

green bean haricot *m* vert

green salad salade *f* verte

grocery store épicerie *f*

guided tour visite *f* guidée

H

ham jambon *m*

hand main *f*

handcuffed menotté *m* / menottée *f*

hangover *(slang)* la gueule de bois (literally: a wooden head)

hay fever rhume *m* des foins

headphones écouteurs *m*

health food store magasin *m* de diététique

heat (in building) chauffage *m*

to help aider

hepatitis hépatite *f*

here ici

herpes herpès *m*

hi salut

hives (allergy) urticaire *f*

hobby passe-temps *m*

honey miel *m*

hostel auberge *m* de jeunesse

hot chaud *m* / chaude *f*

hot chocolate chocolat chaud

hotel hôtel *m*

hour heure *f*

how comment

how long (time) combien de temps

how many combien

how much combien

husband mari *m*

I

ice glace *f*

ice cream glace *f*

iced tea thé *m* glacé

ill malade

in dans

included compris *m* / comprise *f*

inexpensive bon marché *m*, pas cher *m* / chère *f*

information renseignements *m*

information desk bureau *m* des renseignements

inn auberge *m*

insect insecte *m*

to insert insérer
insurance assurance *f*
interesting intéressant *m* / intéressante *f*
International Student Card carte *f* d'étudiant internationale
internet access accès *m* internet
internet café cybercafé *m*
Ireland Irlande *f*
itemized bill note *f* détaillée

J

jacket veste *f*
jail prison *f*
jam confiture *f*
jeans jeans *m*
jelly confiture *f*
jet ski scooter *m* de mer
jewelry bijoux *m*
to jog faire du jogging
juice jus *m*

K

kayak kayak *m*
to keep garder
key clé *f*
kidney rognon *m*
kiss baiser *m*
to kiss embrasser
knife couteau *m*
kosher casher

L

lamb agneau *m*
large grand *m* / grande *f*

last dernier *m* / dernière *f*
late en retard
laundry service service *m* de nettoyage
lawyer avocat *m*
to leave partir
left gauche
leg jambe *f*
lemon citron *m*
lemonade limonade *f*
lesbian lesbienne *f*
less moins
letter lettre *f*
lettuce laitue *f*
lifeguard maître-nageur *m*
light lumière *f*
line queue *f*
lip gloss gloss *m* à lèvres
lips lèvres *m*
lipstick rouge *m* à lèvres
liquor store marchand *m* de vins
liver foie *m*
local cuisine spécialités *f* régionales
local wine vin *m* de pays
lock serrure *f*
to lock enfermer
to log on (computer) se connecter
long long *m* / longue *f*
to look regarder
lost perdu *m* / perdue *f*
love amour *m*
to love aimer

low-calorie pauvre en calories
low-cholesterol pauvre en cholestérol
low-fat pauvre en graisses
low-sodium pauvre en sodium
luggage bagage *m*
lunch déjeuner *m*

M

ma'am madame *f*
mackerel maquereau *m*
magnificent magnifique
main course plat *m*
make-up maquillage *m*
mall centre *m* commercial
man homme *m*
manicure manucure *f*
map plan *m*, carte *f*
market marché *m*
massage massage *m*
matches allumettes *f*
mattress matelas *m*
meal repas *m*, plat *m*
meat viande *f*
mechanic mécanicien *m*
memorial monument *m*
memory card carte *f* mémoire
menu menu *m*
merchandise marchandise *f*
meter (of taxi) compteur *m*
mileage kilométrage *m*
milk lait *m*
milkshake milk shake *m*

mineral water eau *f* minérale
mint menthe *f*
miss mademoiselle *f*
to miss manquer, rater
mistake erreur *f*
moisturizing cream crème *f* hydratante
money argent *m*
moped cyclomoteur *m*, mobylette *f*, vélomoteur *m*
mother mère *f*
motion sickness mal *m* des transports
motorboat canot *m* automobile
mountain-climbing alpinisme *m*
movie film *m*, *(slang)* toile *m*
MP3 player Lecteur *m* MP3
mugging agression *f*
museum musée *m*
mushroom champignon *m*
music musique *f*
mussel moule *f*
mustard moutarde *f*

N

napkin serviette *f*
near (nearby) près, proche
to need avoir besoin (de)
newsstand kiosque *m* à journaux
next prochain *m* / prochaine *f*
night nuit *f*
nightclub boîte *f* (de nuit)
nine neuf

ple téton m

non

sy bruyant m / bruyante f

-smoking area zone f
n-fumeur

e nez m

hing rien

w maintenant

le beach plage f nudiste

O

se obèse

ce bureau m

town vieille ville f

sale en solde m

un m / une f

-way (ticket) aller-simple m

on oignon m

n ouvert m / ouverte f

ra house opéra m

osing team (sports)
dversaire m

nge orange f

rder commander

side dehors

rseas mail l'étranger

ter huître f

P

kage paquet m

nkiller analgésique f

ace palais m

ties culotte f

ts pantalon m

ent parent m

park parc m

party fête f

to party faire la fête

passport passeport m

pastry shop pâtisserie f

to pay payer

pay phone téléphone m public

peanut cacahuète f

pear poire f

peas petits pois m

pebbly de galets m

pedicure pédicure f, soin m des
pieds

pepper poivre m

per day par jour

per hour par heure

per week par semaine

perfume shop parfumerie f

pharmacy pharmacie f

phone téléphone m

to phone téléphoner

phone booth cabine f
téléphonique

phone card télécarte f

photo photo f

pickle cornichon m

pill pilule f

pillow oreiller m

pink rose

pitcher carafe f

plane avion m

plastic surgery chirurgie f
esthétique

plate assiette f

platform quai *m*

play pièce *f* de théâtre

please s'il vous plaît

police police *f* / policiers *m (pl)*

police station commissariat *m*

pork porc *m*

post office bureau *m* de poste

postage tarif *m*

postcard carte *f* postale

potato pomme *f* de terre

powder poudre *f*

prescription ordonnance *f*

program programme *m*

purple violet *m* / violette *f*

purse sac *m* à main

Q

quickly vite

R

rabbit lapin *m*

racetrack hippodrome *m*

rape viol *m*

rate tarif *m*

razor rasoir *m*

receipt reçu *m*

to recommend recommander

red rouge

referee arbitre *m*

refund remboursement *m*

register caisse *f*

to rent louer

to repeat répéter

to report (to police) signaler

reservation réservation *f*

to reserve réserver

restaurant restaurant *m*

restroom toilettes *f*

to return revenir

right droite

right-of-way priorité *f*

to rollerblade faire du roller

roll (bread) petit pain *m*

romantic romantique

room salle *f*

room service service *m* de chambre

round-trip aller-retour *m*

rowing machine rameur *m*

ruins ruines *f*

rum rhum *m*

S

safe coffre-fort *m*

salad salade *f*

salad dressing vinaigrette *f*

sale solde *m*

salmon saumon *m*

(beauty) salon (chez l')esthéticienne

salt sel *m*

sand sable *m*

sanitary napkin serviette *f* hygiénique

sauce sauce *f*

sausage saucisse *f*

savings account compte *m* épargne

schedule les horaires *m*

science science *f*

Scotland Écosse *f*

scrambled eggs oeufs *m* brouillés

screwdriver (alcoholic drink) vodka *f* orange

scumbag ordure *f*

seasoning assaisonnement *m*

seat place *f*, siège *m*

security sécurité *f*

service service *m*

set menu menu *m* à prix fixe

seven sept

sex sexe *m*

sexually transmitted disease (STD) maladie *f* sexuellement transmise (MST)

shampoo shampooing *m*

shirt chemise *f*

shoe chaussure *f*

shop magasin *m*

shopping area rues *f* commerçantes

short (person) petit *m* / petite *f*, **(thing)** court *m* / courte

shorts short *m*

shot (of liquor) *(slang)* verre *m*

shower douche *f*

shrimp crevette *f*

sick malade

sightseeing tour visite *f* touristique

sign panneau *m*

single room chambre *f* à un lit

sink lavabo *m*

sir monsieur

sister sœur

six six

to skateboard faire du skate

skin peau *f*

skinny maigre

skirt jupe *f*

skydiving saut *m* en parachute

sleeper car wagon-lit *m*

sleeping bag sac *m* de couchage

slowly lentement

small petit *m* / petite *f*

small change petite monnaie *f*

to smoke fumer

smoking (section) fumeur

snack bar snack-bar *m*, buffet *m*

snail escargot *m*

sneakers tennis *m*, baskets *m*

soap savon *m*

soccer football *m*

socks chaussettes *f*

soda boisson *f* gazeuse

sodium sodium *m*

sole sole *f*

sore throat mal *m* de gorge

soup soupe *f*

sour acide

souvenir souvenir *m*

sparkling (wine) crémant, mousseux

to speak parler

to spell épeler

spinning vélo *m* sur piste

spoon cuillère *f*

sports store magasin *m* d'articles de sport

stamp timbre *m*

to start commencer

station gare *f*

stationary bike vélo *m* de salle

STD (sexually transmitted disease) MST (maladie sexuellement transmise)

steak steak *m*

to steal voler

stereo chaîne *f*

stolen volé *m* / volée *f*

stomach ventre *m*

to stop arrêter

store magasin *m*

strawberry fraise *f*

student étudiant *m* / étudiante *f*

stunning stupéfiant *m* / stupéfiante *f*

subtitle sous-titre *m*

subway Métro *m*

sugar sucre *m*

suitcase valise *f*

sun soleil *m*

sun block écran *m* total

sunburn coups *m* de soleil

sunglasses lunettes *f* de soleil

suntan lotion crème *f* solaire

superb superbe

supermarket supermarché *m*

to surf faire du surf

surfboard planche *f* de surf

sweet doux *m* / douce *f*

sweetener édulcorant *m*

to swim se baigner, nager, faire de la natation

swim trunks slip *m* de bain

swimming pool piscine *f*

syphilis syphilis *f*

T

table wine vin *m* de table, vin *m* ordinaire

to take (something) prendre

to take (somewhere) emmener

tall grand *m* / grande *f*

tampon tampon *m*

to tattoo tatouer

tax taxe *f*

taxi taxi *m*

tea thé *m*

team équipe *m*

telephone téléphone *m*

telephone card télécarte *f*

television télévision *f*

television set téléviseur *m*

ten dix

tennis tennis *m*

tent tente *f*

theater théâtre *m*

theft cambriolage *m*

thief voleur *m*

thong string *m*

three trois

throat gorge *f*

ticket billet *m*

tight serré *m* / serrée *f*

time temps
timetable les horaires *m*
tire pneu *m*
tired fatigué *m* / fatiguée *f*
tissues mouchoirs *m* en papier
toast pain *m* grillé
today aujourd'hui
toenails ongles *m* des pieds
toilet toilette *f*
toilet paper papier *m* toilette
tomato tomate *f*
tomorrow demain
tonight ce soir
toothpaste dentifrice *m*
tossed salad salade *f* composée
tour excursion *f*, visite *f*
tourist information office office *m* du tourisme
tow truck dépanneuse *f*
towel serviette *f* de bain
tower tour *f*
town ville *f*
town hall hôtel *m* de ville
traditional local dishes spécialités *f* régionales
train train *m*
to translate traduire
travelers checks chèques de voyage
treadmill tapis *m* de course
trip voyage *m*
trousers pantalon *m*
trout truite *f*
truck camion *m*

truffle truffe *f*
T-shirt tee-shirt *m*
tuna thon *m*
to turn off (a machine) éteindre
to turn on (a machine) allumer
twelve douze
two deux

U

ugly laid *m* / laide *f*
umbrella parapluie *m*
to understand comprendre
upset stomach mal *m* de ventre
U.S. États-Unis *m*

V

to validate (a ticket) composter (votre billet)
vanilla vanille *f*
veal veau *m*
vegan végétalien *m* / végétalienne *f*
vegetable salad salade *f* russe
vegetarian végétarien *m* / végétarienne *f*
venereal disease maladie *f* sexuellement transmise (MST)
viewpoint belvédère *m*
vineyard vignoble *m*
vitamin vitamine *f*
vodka vodka *f*
volleyball volley *m*
to vomit vomir

W

to wait attendre
to wake up (se) réveiller
wallet porte-monnaie *m*, portefeuille *m*
war memorial monument *m* aux morts
watch *n* montre *f*
water eau *f*
waterski ski *m* nautique
wax (hair) épilation *f*
webpage page *f* web
week semaine *f*
weekend week-end *m*
weights haltères *m*
what time à quelle heure
when quand
where où
which quel *m* / quelle *f*

whisky whisky *m*
white blanc *m* / blanche *f*
Wi-Fi® area espace *m* Wi-Fi®
wife femme *f*
window fenêtre *f*
wine vin *m*
wine list carte *f* des vins
winery vignoble *m*
withdrawal (of money) retrait *m*
without sans
woman femme *f*
to work marcher
to write écrire

Y

yellow jaune
yes oui
youth hostel auberge *m* de jeunesse